W9-BJK-198

DISCOVERING CAREERS FOR YOUR FUTURE

art

SECOND EDITION

Ferguson
An imprint of Infobase Publishing

Ferguson
An imprint of Infobase Publishing
132 West 31st Street
New York NY 10001

Library of Congress Cataloging-in-Publication Data

Discovering careers for your future. Art. — 2nd ed.
   p. cm.
  Includes bibliographical references and index.
  ISBN-13: 978-0-8160-7276-7
  ISBN-10: 0-8160-7276-0
 1. Art—Vocational guidance—United States—Juvenile literature.
  N6505.D57 2008
  702.3'73—dc22
                     2007037783

Ferguson books are available at special discounts when purchased in bulk quantities for businesses, associations, institutions, or sales promotions. Please call our Special Sales Department in New York at (212) 967-8800 or (800) 322-8755.

You can find Ferguson on the World Wide Web at http://www.fergpubco.com

Text design by Mary Susan Ryan Flynn
Cover design by Jooyoung An

Printed in the United States of America

EB MSRF 10 9 8 7 6 5 4 3 2 1

This book is printed on acid-free paper.

Contents

Introduction

You may not have decided yet what you want to be in the future. And you don't have to decide right away. You do know that right now you are interested in art. Do any of the statements below describe you? If so, you may want to begin thinking about what a career in art might mean for you.

___My favorite class in school is art.
___I enjoy painting and drawing.
___I like to use my hands to make or build things.
___I work hard to make my school reports attractive.
___I make posters for my church or school.
___I enjoy photography.
___I often visit art museums and galleries.
___I make my own jewelry.
___I like making films with my video camera.
___I volunteer to arrange my class bulletin board.
___I arrange the furniture and decorate my own room.
___I spend a lot of time using art and illustration programs on my computer.
___I enjoy drawing cartoons.
___I like to look at art history books.
___I am interested in colors, shapes, and textures.

Discovering Careers for Your Future: Art is a book about careers in art, from animators to special effects technicians. Artists include those who work in two-dimensional art (such as painting and drawing) and three-dimensional art (sculpture), as well as architecture, film, computer and video games, publishing, advertising, fashion, and photography. Some are fine artists, who create works for personal expression and to communicate ideas. Their art is mostly for viewing, such as paintings and sculpture, although often their art is useful as well, such as ceramics. Other artists are commercial artists, who make art for advertising, publishing, public relations, and other business enterprises to attract attention, sell products and services, illustrate ideas, and record events.

This book describes many possibilities for future careers in art. Read through it and see how the different careers are connected. For example, if you are interested in painting and drawing, you will want to read the chapters on artists, cartoonists, conservators and conservation technicians, creative arts therapists, fashion illustrators, and illustrators. If you are interested in photography, you will want to read the chapters on art directors, cinematographers, fashion photographers, photo stylists, photographers, and special effects technicians. Go ahead and explore!

What Do Artists Do?

The first section of each chapter begins with a heading such as "What Animators Do" or "What Graphic Designers Do." This section tells what it's like to work at this job. It also describes typical responsibilities and working conditions. Which artists work in studios? Which ones work at computers in offices? Which artists work on movie sets or at fashion shots? This section answers these and other questions.

How Do I Become an Artist?

The section called "Education and Training" tells you what schooling you need for employment in each job—a high school diploma, training at a junior college, a college degree, or more. It also talks about what high school and college courses you should take to prepare for the field.

How Much Do Artists Earn?

The Earnings section gives the average salary figures for the job described in the chapter. These figures give you a general idea of how much money people with this job can make. Keep in mind that many people really earn more or less than the amounts given here because actual salaries depend on many different things, such as the size of the company, the location of the company, and the amount of education, training, and experience you have. Generally, but not always, larger companies located in major cities pay more than smaller ones in smaller cities and towns, and people with more education, training, and experience earn more. Also remember that these figures are current or recent averages. They will probably be different by the time you are ready to enter the workforce.

What Will the Future be Like for Artists?

The Outlook section discusses the employment outlook for the career: whether the total number of people employed in this career will increase or decrease in the coming years and whether jobs in this field will be easy or hard to find. These predictions are based on economic conditions, the size and makeup of the population, foreign competition, and new technology. Terms such as "about as fast as the average" and "slower than the average," are terms used by the U.S. Department of Labor to describe job growth predicted by government data.

Keep in mind that these predictions are general statements. No one knows for sure what the future will be like. Also remember that the employment outlook is a general statement about an industry and does not necessarily apply to everyone. A determined and talented person may be able to find a job in an industry or career with the worst outlook. And a person without ambition and the proper training will find it difficult to find a job in even a booming industry or career field.

Where Can I Find More Information?

Each chapter includes a sidebar called "For More Info." It lists resources that you can contact to find out more about the field and careers in the field. You will find names, addresses, phone numbers, e-mail addresses, and Web sites of art-oriented associations and organizations.

Extras

Every chapter has a few extras. There are photos that show artists in action. There are sidebars and notes on ways to explore the field, fun facts, profiles of people in the field, or lists of Web sites and books that might be helpful. At the end of the book you will find a glossary, an index, and a Browse and Learn More section. The glossary gives brief definitions of words that relate to education, career training, or employment that you may be unfamiliar with. The index includes all the job titles mentioned in the book. The Browse and Learn More section lists general art books and Web sites to explore.

It's not too soon to think about your future. We hope you discover several possible career choices in the art field. Happy hunting!

Animators

What Animators Do

Animators design the cartoons you see on television, at the movies, and on the Internet. They also create the digital effects for many films and commercials. Making a big animated film, such as *Ratatouille, Finding Nemo,* or *The Incredibles* requires a team of many creative people. Each animator on the team works on one small part of the film. On a small production, animators may be involved in many different aspects of the project's development.

An animated film begins with a script. *Screenwriters* plan the story line, or plot, and write it with dialogue and narration.

Words to Learn

animatic a kind of digital storyboard that allows animations to be viewed on a video monitor

fps frames per second; in general, the higher the number of frames, the better the animation will be

kinematics animating a model to move the way a human moves

layers used in complex animation to help manipulate objects; different objects can be assigned different layers and then moved independently

modeling the process used to make animated objects from a real object; animators use models to help them envision an object and figure out how to draw its movements on flat paper

rendering making a character or an inanimate object seem lifelike; artists use color, shadow, texture, and light to render

storyboarding an outline of an animation in a series of drawings in multiple frames

EXPLORING

○ Practice sketching. Carry a sketch-pad around in order to quickly capture images and gestures that seem interesting to you.

○ There are many computer animation software programs available that teach basic principles and techniques. Use these to hone your skills.

○ Participate in school or community art clubs. Draw posters to publicize activities, such as sporting events, dances, and meetings.

○ Some video cameras have stop-motion buttons that allow you to take a series of still shots. You can use this feature to experiment with claymation and other stop-motion techniques.

Designers read the script and decide how the film should look—should it be realistic, futuristic, or humorous? They then draw some of the characters and backgrounds. These designs are then passed on to a *storyboard artist* who illustrates the whole film in a series of frames, similar to a very long comic strip. Based on this storyboard, an artist can then create a detailed layout.

The most common form of animation is cell animation. Animators examine the script, the storyboard, and the layout, and begin to prepare the finished artwork frame by frame, or cell by cell, on a combination of paper and transparent plastic sheets. Some animators create the "key" drawings—these are the drawings that capture the characters' main expressions and gestures at important parts in the plot. Other animators create the "in-between" drawings—the drawings that fill in the spaces between one key drawing and the next. The thousands of final black and white cells are then scanned into a computer. (A television cartoon has 25 to 30 images per second.) With computer programs, animators add color, special effects, and other details.

In stop-motion animation, an object, such as a clay creature or doll is photographed, moved slightly, and photographed again. The process is repeated hundreds of thousands of times. Movies such as *Chicken Run* were animated this way. In computer or digital animation, the animator

The Internet Connection

You'll find lots of animation information on the Internet. Try these Web sites:

About.com: Animation
http://animation.about.com

Animation: Creating Movement Frame by Frame
http://www.oscars.org/teachersguide/animation/

Animation Artist
http://animationartist.digitalmedianet.com

Animation Magazine
http://www.animationmagazine.net

creates all the images directly on the computer screen. Computer programs can create effects like shadows, reflections, distortions, and dissolves.

Education and Training

Art and drawing classes will prepare you for a career in animation. Photography classes can help you to develop visual composition skills. English composition and literature classes will help you develop creative writing skills. Computer classes are important for learning to use art-related software, such as illustration, graphics, and animation programs.

A college education isn't required, but there are a number of animation programs offered at universities and art institutes across the country. You may choose to pursue a bachelor's and/or a master's of fine art degree, or a Ph.D. in computer animation, digital art, graphic design, or art. Some of today's top computer animators are self-taught or have learned their skills on the job.

FOR MORE INFO

For information about animated films and digital effects, visit the AWN's Web site, which includes feature articles, a list of schools, and a career section.

Animation World Network (AWN)
6525 Sunset Boulevard, Garden Suite 10
Hollywood, CA 90028-7212
Tel: 323-606-4200
E-mail: info@awn.com
http://www.awn.com

For an animation archive and information on children's animation workshops, visit the society's Web site.

International Animated Film Society
2114 West Burbank Boulevard
Burbank, CA 91506-1232
Tel: 818-842-8330
E-mail: info@asifa-hollywood.org
http://www.asifa-hollywood.org

Earnings

Animators earn from $1,200 to $2,000 a week on average. Very experienced and successful animators, designers, and art directors can earn more than $1 million a year. A salary survey conducted by *Animation World* reported that cell painters start at about $750 a week; animation checkers, $930 a week; and story sketchers, $1,500 a week. According to *U.S. News & World Report*, animators, depending on their experience, can earn from $800 to $1,800 a week. Top animators can command weekly fees of about $6,500 or more.

Outlook

Opportunities in this field are expected to grow about as fast as the average, according to the U.S. Department of Labor. Animated films continue to make millions of dollars at the box office. Cable television is also producing more and more successful animated series for both children and adults. No matter how many animation projects there are, however, it likely will remain very difficult to get a job at a studio. Pixar, the studio that created *Finding Nemo, Ratatouille,* and *Toy Story,* receives about 2,000 reels (short films demonstrating the work of animators) a year from hopeful job candidates. Of this number, the studio will hire fewer than 100 animators.

Art Directors

What Art Directors Do

Art directors are in charge of all images that appear in print (newspapers, books, magazines, and advertisements) and on screen (television, movies, videos, and the Web). Art directors work at advertising agencies, film studios, publishing companies, theater companies, and other organizations that produce or use visual elements, such as photography, illustrations, props, costumes, and sets. Art directors hire illustrators, photographers, animators, set and costume designers, and models and find existing illustrations and photos that can be used for projects. Sometimes they combine new and existing art to create the needed visual effect.

Some art directors work with printed material, such as newspapers, magazines, and books. They are experts in arranging the text, pictures, and other visual elements, as well as using color, photography, and different kinds of lettering called typefaces. Art directors work on television broadcasts, films, commercials, and Web sites. They know filmmaking and video production techniques, computer graphics, and animation, depending on their specialty. Art directors also work on stage productions. They manage the team of lighting, set, costume, makeup, and sound designers.

Award Winners

Here are recent Oscar winners for art direction:

2006: Eugenio Caballero, *Pan's Labyrinth*

2005: John Myhre, *Memoirs of a Geisha*

2004: Dante Ferretti, *The Aviator*

2003: Grant Major, *The Lord of the Rings: The Return of the King*

2002: John Myhre, *Chicago*

2001: Catherine Martin, *Moulin Rouge*

2000: Tim Yip, *Crouching Tiger, Hidden Dragon*

1999: Rick Heinrichs, *Sleepy Hollow*

1998: Martin Childs, *Shakespeare in Love*

1997: Peter Lamont, *Titanic*

EXPLORING

○ Develop your own artistic talent by reading books and practicing drawing skills or taking art classes.

○ Visit art galleries and museums. Study paintings, as well as magazines, motion pictures, videos, or commercials. Notice color, composition, balance, mood, and other visual elements.

○ Work on the staff of your school newspaper, magazine, or yearbook.

Art directors for film, television, and other broadcast media usually submit several rough drawings, called storyboards, which show step-by-step what the filmed piece will look like when it is finished. Then the storyboards are coordinated with the script and music, and the production begins. In television commercials, the art director is involved in choosing actors, editing the film, and selecting the music. Every stage of the film is reviewed by the art director until it is ready for broadcast or reproduction.

In print media, art directors sketch a design of what the page will look like. They block out areas for text, artwork, and other graphics. The art director then selects illustrators, photographers, or graphic designers to create the finished art for the project. A *production editor* or *graphic designer* puts the finished pieces together into a final form, usually a computer layout file. The art director sees every part of the process and gives approval or orders changes. Once the art director is satisfied with the final proof, the project is ready to be printed.

Education and Training

To prepare for a career as an art director, concentrate on art and computer classes, as well as math. Most art directors have at least a bachelor's degree, usually in graphic design or fine art. A few go on to earn master's degrees. Film art directors can earn a degree in film, directing, animation, or cinematography.

To Be a Successful Art Director, You Should . . .

- be creative and imaginative
- be able to work with all sorts of specialized equipment and computer software
- have the ability to work well with different types of people
- be able to handle stress and pressure
- have good time management skills

Art directors rarely start out as art directors. Their first jobs may be as graphic designers, production assistants, or illustrators. As they gain experience and learn the ins and outs of the print or film industries, they move into higher positions until they become art directors.

Earnings

The average salary for art directors was about $68,100 in 2006, according to the U.S. Department of Labor. Entry-level art directors earned $37,920 a year, while very experienced art directors can earn more than $135,000 a year.

Outlook

Opportunities for well-qualified art directors should continue to be good. Competition for jobs will be strong, though. It takes many years assisting in design and layout before you can become an art director.

Employment in the general area of visual art is expected to grow about as fast as the average, according to the U.S.

FOR MORE INFO

For industry information, contact
American Advertising Federation
1101 Vermont Avenue NW, Suite 500
Washington, DC 20005-6306
Tel: 800-999-2231
E-mail: aaf@aaf.org
http://www.aaf.org

American Institute of Graphic Arts
164 Fifth Avenue
New York, NY 10010-5901
Tel: 212-807-1990
http://www.aiga.org

Art Directors Club
106 West 29th Street
New York, NY 10001-5301
Tel: 212-643-1440
E-mail: info@adcglobal.org
http://www.adcglobal.org

*For information on art directors who are
employed in the motion picture industry,
contact*
**Art Directors Guild & Scenic, Title,
and Graphic Artists**
11969 Ventura Boulevard, 2nd Floor
Studio City, CA 91604-2619
Tel: 818-762-9995
http://www.artdirectors.org

Department of Labor. One area that shows particularly good promise for growth is the retail industry, since more and more large retail establishments—especially catalog houses—will be employing in-house advertising art directors.

Artists

What Artists Do

Visual arts are roughly divided into three categories: commercial art, fine art, and craft. Commercial art is art used by advertising, publishing, public relations, and other businesses to attract attention, sell products and services, illustrate ideas, send messages, and record events. *Commercial artists* include *illustrators, graphic designers, art directors,* and *photographers.* Most

Words to Learn

broken color colors laid next to each other and blended by the eye of the viewer; instead of mixing red and blue on a palette to make purple, red and blue are placed next to each other on the canvas

drybrush a technique in which thick paint is stroked lightly over a dry surface; it produces a broken or mottled effect

glaze a film of transparent paint applied over a solid color, giving a luminous, rich effect

impasto a thick application of paint to a canvas or panel; the marks of the brush or palette knife can be seen plainly

scumble an application of opaque paint over a different color of paint; the original color is not covered entirely, giving an uneven effect

stippling the technique of applying small dots of paint to a surface to build up tonal areas or textures

underpainting a preliminary painting on the painting surface. Using tones of one color, the artist makes an underpainting to establish the basic shapes, values, and overall composition of a painting

wash a thin layer of paint spread evenly over a broad area

wet-in-wet a technique in which fresh paint is applied on top of or into wet paint already on the support this technique is used with watercolors and oils

EXPLORING

○ Use library resources to learn about the history of art, artistic techniques, and methods.

○ Making art is something you can do on your own. You can sharpen your skills and find new ideas by painting, sketching, sculpting, or taking pictures, for example, on a regular basis.

○ Most elementary, middle, and high schools offer classes in art. Many arts associations and community centers also offer beginning classes in various types of art for the general public.

○ Visit museums and galleries often to view the work of other artists.

commercial art combines pictures with text, and artists use a variety of media to create two-dimensional works that can be easily reproduced. Computers are an important tool commercial artists use to design pages, choose type, scan photos and artwork, create illustrations, and manipulate photos.

Fine art is art created more for personal expression than financial gain. Usually the art comes from the artist's own ideas rather than from an employer's or client's needs. *Painters* use oil, acrylic, or watercolor paints on various surfaces, such as paper, canvas, wood, or plaster. *Sculptors* use materials such as clay, metal, wood, stone, papier mâché, and plastic to build, carve, sandblast, cast, or mold three-dimensional forms. *Calligraphers* use ink, pencil, paper, books, wood, even gold and silver. *Printmakers* make prints from carved blocks, etched plates, and silk screens. *Ceramic artists* use clay and glazes to create sculpture, functional pottery, beads, tiles, or architectural decorations. Other fine artists use airbrush, pastels, charcoal,

Profile: Pablo Picasso (1881–1973)

Picasso was a Spanish-born painter and sculptor. He was one of the artists who originated the style known as Cubism. His abstract paintings made him one of the most controversial and influential artists of the twentieth century.

Picasso was born Pablo Ruiz Blasco. He studied with his father, an art teacher, and in Barcelona and Madrid. Around 1900, he began to sign his works with his mother's surname, Picasso. During his long career, he painted and sculpted in many styles. Later in his life, he also became interested in ceramics and made hundreds of pieces of pottery.

collage, or mixed media, to name a few of the more traditional media. Only a few fine artists make a living from their art. Most earn income from other occupations while pursuing their art in their free time. The most common way for fine artists to show and sell their art is through galleries.

The field of visual arts also includes craft, sometimes called handcraft, or arts and crafts. Craft refers to art objects that usually (but not always) have a function. Needle arts, jewelry making, basketry, wood carving, mosaic, some ceramics, and bookbinding are examples of crafts. *Crafters* sell their works through retail stores, fairs, catalogs, the Internet, and galleries.

Education and Training

Artists should have some natural artistic ability and also should be creative and imaginative. Even very talented people will have difficulty becoming professional artists without education, however. Most artists go to art school to help develop their skills and learn new ones. Many colleges and universities offer degrees in fine art, applied (commercial) art, and art history. Those artists who study in a college or university must also study history, English, and computer science, as these studies help broaden their historical and cultural views and add to their creative work. Most art schools offer fine art and commercial art programs, where you can choose to specialize in graphic design, animation, photography, or film.

Earnings

There is no average salary for an artist. Many artists set their own hours and prices for their work and most artists have other full- or part-time work that

An artist paints in her studio. (Larry Williams, Corbis)

provides them with a steady income. Some artists give private classes or teach in an art school or college.

According to the U.S. Department of Labor, salaried, full-time artists in 2006 earned an average of $41,970 a year. Salaries ranged from less than $18,350 to more than $79,390 a year. Some internationally known artists may earn millions of dollars for their work, but this is rare.

Outlook

Because artists are usually self-employed, much of their success depends on the amount and type of work they create and their ability to sell it.

Employment for visual artists is expected to grow about as fast as the average, according to the U.S. Department of Labor. Talented artists who have a wide range of skills, including computer skills, will have the best job opportunities.

FOR MORE INFO

For an overview of craft art, useful publications, and a list of craft shows and markets, visit the council's Web site
American Craft Council
72 Spring Street, 6th Floor
New York, NY 10012-4019
Tel: 212-274-0630
E-mail: council@craftcouncil.org
http://www.craftcouncil.org

For general information on the study of the arts, contact
National Art Education Association
1916 Association Drive
Reston, VA 20191-1590
Tel: 703-860-8000
http://www.naea-reston.org

The National Sculpture Society is the oldest organization of professional sculptors in the United States. You can view the work of members at its Web site.
National Sculpture Society
237 Park Avenue
New York, NY 10017-0010
http://www.nationalsculpture.org

To view the work of sculptors, visit the following Web site
Sculptors Guild
110 Greene Street, Suite 601
New York, NY 10012-3838
Tel: 212-431-5669
E-mail: sculptorsguild@gmail.com
http://www.sculptorsguild.org

Cartoonists

What Cartoonists Do

Cartoonists draw the illustrations for comic strips, political cartoons, comic books, magazines, greeting cards, and advertisements. Sometimes cartoons are meant to entertain, as in comic strips. Other times they send a political or social message, as in editorial cartoons in a newspaper. Sometimes cartoonists tell a longer story, as in a comic book. Still other times, cartoonists are hired to sell a product, as in advertisements.

Most cartoonists have very individual approaches to their work. Some get ideas from their own experience, much like a stand-up comedian. Others get ideas from events or people in their neighborhoods and towns. Some find humor or satire in news events that happen around the world.

Cartoonists make sketches and "rough out" their ideas. These sketches eventually lead to a final drawing. The final drawing is often done lightly in pencil and then cartoonists

Profile: Charles M. Schulz (1922–2000)

Charles M. Schulz created the comic strip *Peanuts*. The strip appeals to young and old alike. Its child characters, including Charlie Brown, Lucy, and Linus, combine traits of children and adults. Another main character is Snoopy, Charlie Brown's thinking dog.

Schulz was born in Minneapolis, Minnesota. He took his first drawing lessons in the early 1940s and after army service became a cartoonist. By 1950 he had created the *Peanuts* strip, which eventually appeared in more than 1,000 newspapers in North America and some 40 foreign countries, in a dozen different languages. Schulz also published many books portraying the comic strip characters. A musical, *You're a Good Man, Charlie Brown* (1967), and a number of television specials were based on *Peanuts*.

EXPLORING

○ Read comic strips, comic books, and other cartoons. Pay special attention to the drawings and the dialogue or story line.
○ Keep a sketch book handy and practice drawing every day. Over time you will develop your own special characters and style.
○ Submit some of your cartoons to your school newspaper. Ask the editors to use you as a regular cartoonist. Draw posters for school or sporting events, dances, or meetings.

ink in the lines. They add lettering and sometimes color by hand.

Some cartoonists use computers to add shading or color to the drawings. They use a scanner to scan the drawing, then use an illustration software program to complete it.

Most cartoonists are freelancers, which means they work in their own studios and set their own hours. They sell their cartoons to one or more clients.

Education and Training

To be a cartoonist, you need to develop art and drawing skills. English composition and literature classes will help you develop creative writing skills.

You don't necessarily need a college education to be a cartoonist, but you should have some formal art training. Political science, history, and social studies classes give you different views of life and can be a good source of ideas.

To Be a Successful Cartoonist, You Should . . .

○ be creative and have artistic talent
○ be able to create concepts and images that the public will respond to
○ have a good sense of humor
○ be flexible regarding assignments from employers

Many cartoonists begin their careers by selling cartoons to small publications, such as community newspapers. Another way to start your career is to put together a collection, called a portfolio, of your best work and show it to publishers, syndicates, or advertising agencies. Your success depends on how much the public likes your work.

Earnings

Freelance cartoonists earn anywhere from $50 to $1,200 per assignment. Well-known artists earn much higher fees. Comic strip cartoonists are usually paid according to the number of newspapers that carry their strip and they can earn $100,000 or more a year.

Those who create very popular strips and characters may share in the profits of merchandise such as toys, dolls, calendars, and games inspired by the strip. Cartoonists can earn high fees for large full-color illustrations or an advertising campaign.

FOR MORE INFO

Visit the society's Web site to read "How to be a Cartoonist."
National Cartoonists Society
341 North Maitland Avenue, Suite 130
Maitland, FL 32751-4761
Tel: 407-647-8839
http://www.reuben.org

For career information, contact
Society of Illustrators
128 East 63rd Street
New York, NY 10021-7303
Tel: 212-838-2560
E-mail: info@societyillustrators.org
http://www.societyillustrators.org

Outlook

Opportunities in this field are expected to grow about as fast as the average, according to the U.S. Department of Labor. It can be very difficult to earn a steady wage and work full time in this career. The most opportunities will be with advertising departments or graphic arts agencies. Having your work published in magazines and newspapers will require great persistence. The syndicates (those companies that sell strips to newspapers) reject thousands of artist portfolios every year. Small local newspapers are a good place to start.

Ceramic Artists

What Ceramic Artists Do

Ceramic artists, also known as *potters, ceramists, sculptors,* and *clay artists,* work with clay to make both art objects and functional objects. Clay is found in the earth beneath rich topsoil and layers of rock. There are many different types of clay that have different colors and textures when they harden. Some ceramic artists build objects by hand, which allows them to create more free-form designs. Hand-building techniques include the coil and slab methods. In the coil method, the artist rolls out long snakes of clay and coils them to form shapes. Slabs are made in much the same way you would roll out a pie crust. Slip, which is clay diluted with water, is used

Profile: Josiah Wedgwood (1730–1795)

English potter Josiah Wedgwood is noted for the beauty and perfection of his ware and for his leadership in making pottery one of England's important industries. He introduced and frequently used the shade of blue we now call Wedgwood blue. Wedgwood ware is found in many private collections and in museums.

Among Wedgwood's creations are queen's ware, a fine, cream-colored earthenware; basalt, a black stoneware; rosso antico, a red stoneware decorated with black figures in relief; and jasper, an unglazed porcelain in white or soft colors, decorated with cameo-like designs in white. Jasper was Wedgwood's last and perhaps greatest creation, and the most widely used and imitated of his wares.

as a kind of glue to hold the coils or slabs together. Other ceramic artists use a potter's wheel to create symmetrical objects. Another method of making ceramics involves making or using molds. A mold can be used to make large quantities of identical items. All clay objects must be allowed to dry and then they must be heated, or fired, in a kiln at high temperatures. Firing the clay makes it hard and permanent. After firing, the artist can apply glazes and fire the objects again.

Ceramic artists sometimes specialize in making beads, tiles, or architectural decorations. *Production potters* make household wares, such as matching dinner plates, cups, and saucers. Production potters also make vases, bowls, and other pieces. These artists might work alone in a studio, or they might set up a large workshop that employs several people.

EXPLORING

○ Experiment with clay on your own. Different kinds of clay are available at art stores. You will have to find someplace with a kiln that will fire it for you. You might also experiment with clays that air dry or with polymer clays. You can use many of the same hand-building techniques as for natural clay. Most polymer clays can be fired in just a few minutes in a regular oven set at a low temperature.

○ Take a ceramics class. Check with your community arts programs or a local art school for course offerings.

○ Take art classes in which you can work on three-dimensional projects, such as model-building and sculpture.

Education and Training

If you want to be a ceramic artist, you have to be willing to get your hands dirty. Pottery classes are usually offered for people of all ages. Like other artists, those who work with clay often learn the basics of their craft in formal art programs with experienced artists and then they practice their own styles. In class, you learn how to work with clay, how to build shapes with your hands and with a potter's wheel, and how to glaze and fire what you make. There are no formal

All About Clay

○ **Kaolin**, or **china clay**, is for making pure white porcelain or china. It is seldom used by itself—other materials are added to it to make it more workable and to lower the kiln temperature necessary to produce a hard, dense product. Genuine translucent porcelains are fired between 2,300°F and 2,550°F.

○ **Ball clays** contain more iron, are more fusible, and are much more plastic than kaolin clays. Ball clays and kaolin are often combined. Ball clays are so named because of the practice in England of forming the damp clay in the mines into large balls that could be rolled up onto wagons for transport. Ball clays are fired at about 1,800°F and are a light gray or light buff color.

○ **Stoneware clays** vary widely in color, plasticity, and firing range (1,200°F to 2,400°F). Their color ranges from a very light gray or buff to a darker gray or brown. Stoneware clays are sedimentary clays. There is no sharp distinction between stoneware clays and what are called fire clays or sagger clays.

○ **Earthenware clay**, or **common clay**, contains enough iron and other mineral impurities to cause the clay to harden at about 1,750°F to 2,000°F. Raw earthenware is red, brown, greenish, or gray. Fired earthenware varies from pink to buff to tan, red, brown, or black. Most of the pottery the world over has been made of earthenware clay.

education requirements for becoming a ceramic artist. Many work as apprentices in studios of large production companies for several years. To become a professional ceramic artist, it is wise to earn a bachelor's degree in fine arts, with a major in ceramic art and design.

Earnings

There are no standard earnings for ceramic artists who work on their own. It's difficult, especially starting out, to earn a living just from selling your work. It takes many years to create a style and build a demand for your designs.

If you decide that you want to earn steady pay, you can work for an established potter or a large ceramics manufacturing firm. This type of job might pay $25,000 to $35,000 a year.

Outlook

It is very hard to predict whether ceramic artists will enjoy success and recognition in the near future. However, there are good signs that ceramics as an art form has the potential to become well recognized. There are many books, videos, magazines, and Web sites on the subject, along with workshops, conferences, and competitions throughout the world. Ceramic artists gather to show their work, work together, and teach

FOR MORE INFO

For general information on ceramic arts study, contact
National Art Education Association
1916 Association Drive
Reston, VA 20191-1590
Tel: 703-860-8000
http://www.naea-reston.org

This association supports established and emerging artists and arts organizations. For information on art programs, contact your state agency, or
National Assembly of State Arts Agencies

1029 Vermont Avenue NW, 2nd Floor
Washington, DC 20005-3517
Tel: 202-347-6352
E-mail: nasaa@nasaa-arts.org
http://www.nasaa-arts.org

For education information, contact
National Council on Education for the Ceramic Arts
77 Erie Village Square, Suite 280
Erie, CO 80516-6996
Tel: 866-266-2322
E-mail: office@nceca.net
http://www.nceca.net

Ceramic artists must not be afraid to get a little dirty as they create art. Their work clothes often get splotched, caked, and stiff, and their hands get covered in clay. (PhotoDisc)

others. Many have made names for themselves in the art world and are valued as artists. Although most of our dishes today are mass-produced with machines and molds, there is still a market for handmade pieces.

Cinematographers

What Cinematographers Do

Cinematographers run the cameras during the making of a film or video. They work closely with directors, actors, and members of the film crew. Cinematographers work on feature films, educational films, industrial training films, documentaries, and commercials. Specific job duties depend on the size of the production. For a documentary with a small crew, a cinematographer may set up the lighting and camera equipment and direct the movements of the actors. For a larger production, the cinematographer might concentrate solely on running the camera, while a team of assistants helps out with loading and unloading film and setting up the equipment.

Cinematographers begin work on a film project by reading the script. They discuss with the director how to film each scene. They decide whether to film from across the room, or up close to the actors. They decide on camera angles, how the camera moves, and how to frame and light each scene. Cinematographers also have a great deal of technical knowledge about film, which helps them decide which cameras, film, and filters to use. Cinematographers are also in charge of the film crew. They hire various assistants and give them

Award Winners

Here are recent Oscar winners for cinematography:

2006: Guillermo Navarro, *Pan's Labyrinth*

2005: Dion Beebe, *Memoirs of a Geisha*

2004: Robert Richardson, *The Aviator*

2003: Russell Boyd, *Master and Commander: The Far Side of the World*

2002: Conrad L. Hall, *Road to Perdition*

2001: Andrew Lesnie, *The Lord of the Rings: The Fellowship of the Ring*

2000: Peter Pau, *Crouching Tiger, Hidden Dragon*

1999: Conrad L. Hall, *American Beauty*

1998: Janusz Kaminski, *Saving Private Ryan*

1997: Russell Carpenter, *Titanic*

EXPLORING

○ Read magazines, such as American *Cinematographer*, *Daily Variety*, *Holly-wood Reporter*, and *Cinefex*, to learn more about filmmaking.

○ Watch as many movies as you can. Study them closely for the styles of the filmmakers.

○ The documentary, *Visions of Light*, is a good introduction to some of the finest cinematography in the history of film.

○ If you have access to a 16 mm camera, a camcorder, or a digital camera, you can experiment with composition, lighting, and other skills.

○ Check with your school's media center or journalism department about filming school events.

detailed instructions on how to film each scene.

Cinematographers work both indoors and outdoors. They sometimes spend several months on location away from home. When working on smaller productions, there may be a limited budget and a smaller film crew, so cinematographers may have to load and unload film from the camera, set up tripods, and carry the camera long distances. They participate in long hours of rehearsal before they actually start to film a scene. Although all their work is behind the scenes, cinematographers play an important part in the appearance and the success of the final film.

Education and Training

Art and photography courses can help you understand the basics of lighting and composition. When you get to high school, take broadcast journalism or media courses that teach camera operation and video production.

A college degree is not always necessary to find a position as a cinematographer. Many cinematographers, though, get that valuable experience during their college studies. There are many colleges and art schools that offer programs in film or cinematography.

Your training should include all aspects of camera operations and lighting. It is important to practice working on a team. You must be able to give directions as well as follow them.

Earnings

When starting out, apprentice film-makers may make no money. Since they usually are hired one film at a time, there may be periods of unpaid time between assignments. As you gain experience, you will begin to find more jobs and earn more. According to the U.S. Department of Labor, camera operators (a category that includes cinematographers) earned an average of $40,060 a year in 2006. Well-established cinematographers working on big-budget productions can make well over $1 million a year, but very few cinematographers earn that much.

Outlook

A large number of people want to work in the movie industry. This means that there are far more qualified cinematographers than there are job openings. If you are skilled and well trained, you should find positions, but it could take a long time before you find work in industry hotspots such as Los Angeles or New York.

You may find better opportunities working on TV commercials, documentaries, or educational films. Cinematographers of the future will be working more closely with special

A cinematographer visualizes a shot. (Joe Sohm, The Image Works)

It's a Fact

○ The first Oscar winners in the category of cinematography were Charles Rosher and Karl Struss for *Sunrise* (1927/28).

○ In 1939, the Academy of Motion Picture Arts and Sciences began to give separate awards for black-and-white and color cinematography. That year, Gregg Toland won in the black-and-white category for *Wuthering Heights* and Ernest Haller and Ray Rennahan won in the color category for *Gone With the Wind.*

○ The last award for black-and-white cinematography was awarded to Haskell Wexler for *Who's Afraid of Virginia Woolf?* in 1966.

○ Only one cinematographer has won four Oscars: Leon Shamroy for *The Black Swan* (1942), *Wilson* (1944), *Leave Her to Heaven* (1945), and *Cleopatra* (1963).

To Be a Successful Cinematographer, You Should . . .

○ be creative and have artistic vision

○ have strong communication skills

○ have good decision-making skills

○ be willing to work long hours in order to meet production deadlines

○ be willing to continuously learn about technological innovations in the industry

effects experts. Computer technology can create effects more easily and cheaply. Cinematographers will have to approach a film with an understanding of which shots can be made digitally and which will need traditional methods of filmmaking.

FOR MORE INFO

For information about colleges with film and television programs of study, and to read interviews with filmmakers, visit the AFI's Web site.

American Film Institute (AFI)
2021 North Western Avenue
Los Angeles, CA 90027-1657
Tel: 323-856-7600
http://www.afionline.org

The ASC's Web site has articles from American Cinematographer *magazine, industry news, and a tips and tricks for cinematographers section.*

American Society of Cinematographers (ASC)
PO Box 2230
Hollywood, CA 90078-2230
Tel: 800-448-0145
http://www.theasc.com

Computer and Video Game Designers

What Computer and Video Game Designers Do

Computer and video game designers create the games played on computers and televisions and in arcades. They think up new game ideas, including sound effects, characters, story lines, and graphics. Some designers work full time for game companies. Other video game designers work as freelancers, making the games in their own studios and then selling their ideas and programs to production companies.

Each game must have a story as well as graphics and sound that will entertain and challenge the players. A game begins with careful planning and preparation. Designers write scripts and sketch storyboards, which are frame-by-frame drawings of the game's events. They must decide how the characters and places should look, and make notes on sound effects and other features.

Designers use computer programs, or write their own programs to assemble text, art, and sound into a digital video.

Types of Computer Games

3D games games that feature 3D environments and usually include action and shooting

adventure games that are puzzle-based

edutainment games that combine educational elements with game elements

fighting games games that feature hand-to-hand combat

god games games that allow the player to control outcomes

platform games vertical-scrolling screen games

retro games games, such as Atari classics, that are recreated on a new platform

role-playing games games that require building a character

shooters games in which the player shoots at targets

simulation games that put the player in a seemingly real situation

sports games strategy games based on soccer, football, tennis, baseball, and other sports

EXPLORING

○ Write your own stories, puzzles, and games to work on your story-telling and problem-solving skills.

○ Read magazines like *Computer Graphics World* (http://www.cgw.com) and *Game Developer* (http://www.gdmag.com). They have articles about digital video and other technical and design information.

○ Try to design easy games, or experiment with games that have an editor. Games like Klik & Play, Empire, and Doom allow you to modify them to create new circumstances.

There is a long process of reviewing and trial-and-error to correct problems and smooth rough spots. Designers usually create a basic game and then design several levels of difficulty for beginning to advanced players. It takes from about 6 to 18 months to design a computer or video game.

Designing computer games often requires a whole team of workers, including programmers, artists, musicians, writers, and animators. Computer and video game designers have a unique combination of highly technical skills and vivid, creative imaginations.

Education and Training

If you want to be a computer and video game designer, you need to learn many different computer skills, including programming. Art, literature, and music classes can help you explore your creativity and develop your own style.

To Be a Successful Computer and Video Game Designer, You Should . . .

○ love playing computer and video games

○ be creative and imaginative

○ stay up to date with ever-changing computer technology

○ have good communication skills in order to work well with programmers, writers, artists, musicians, electronics engineers, production workers, and others

○ be able to work under deadline pressure

Did You Know?

○ Thirty-one percent of game players are under the age of 18.

○ Sixty-two percent of game players are male.

○ The most popular computer game genres (by units sold) in 2005 were strategy (30.8 percent), family and children's (19.8 percent), shooter (14.4 percent), and role-playing (12.4 percent).

○ The most popular video game genres (by units sold) in 2005 were action (30.1 percent), sports (17.3 percent), racing (11.1 percent), and children and family entertainment (9.3 percent).

Sources: Entertainment Software Association, The NPD Group/Point of Sale Information

You don't necessarily need a college degree to be a game designer, but most companies prefer to hire those with a bachelor's degree. Many schools now offer training programs specifically for designing computer games.

Earnings

Computer and video game designers earn between $30,000 and $95,000 per year. Earnings depend on how much experience you have, where you live, the size of the company you work for, and whether you earn bonuses and royalties (a percentage of profits from each game that is sold).

Outlook

The computer and video game industry is growing quickly, with more and more companies hiring skilled people at many levels. Because the industry is fairly new, it is difficult to estimate exactly how many people work as game designers. About 219,000 people work in the computer and video game industry as a whole. Designers should find good opportunities for jobs in the next 10 years as companies try to keep up with the demand for new games.

FOR MORE INFO

For industry information, contact
Entertainment Software Association
575 Seventh Street NW, Suite 300
Washington, DC 20004-1611
E-mail: esa@theesa.com
http://www.theesa.com

For a list of colleges that offer game design programs and comprehensive career information, including Breaking In:

Preparing For Your Career in Games, visit the IGDA's Web site
International Game Developers Association (IGDA)
19 Mantua Road
Mt. Royal, NJ 08061-1006
Tel: 856-423-2990
E-mail: contact@igda.org
http://www.igda.org

Conservators and Conservation Technicians

What Conservators and Conservation Technicians Do

Conservators and conservation technicians examine and judge the condition of artifacts and art objects. These objects may include natural objects, or human-made objects. Conservation workers are employed in museums, historical societies, or state institutions. They usually specialize in a particular area of work, such as the preservation of books and paper, photographs, paintings, textiles, or wooden objects. Other conservators specialize in archaeological or ethnographical (human culture) materials.

The main job of conservators is to conserve or preserve items so that we can learn from them and continue to study them. They decide on the best environment for the artifact to be stored and preserved. Areas that are too hot or too cold or that are high in humidity can cause the item further damage. A conservator's tools can include microscopes and cameras, including equipment for specialized processes such as infrared and ultraviolet photography, and X-ray processes.

Conservation technicians help conservators preserve and restore artifacts and art objects. They may perform

Tips for Handling Artifacts and Artwork

○ Always wear gloves.

○ Support the base of the object. Do not lift or carry the object by its handles or appendages.

○ When moving objects with multiple parts, move only one part of the object at a time.

○ Always set the object on a padded surface in its most stable position.

A conservator restores a fresco painting in the Sistine Chapel. (Vittoriano Rastelli, Corbis)

physical and chemical tests. They may also devise safe ways to clean artifacts. If an object is damaged, conservation technicians may repair it.

Education and Training

You can begin to prepare for a career in historic conservation by concentrating on art, science, and social science classes.

In the past, most conservation workers learned their craft as apprentices with experienced conservators. Today, most conservators have graduate training. First you must earn a bachelor's degree that includes classes in science (especially chemistry), the humanities (art, history, archaeology, and anthropology), and studio art. Then you go on to earn a graduate degree in conservation of art and historic works.

Earnings

The average salary for a chief art museum conservator is about $75,000. Senior conservators earn $40,000 to $65,000 a year.

To Be a Successful Conservator or Conservation Technician, You Should . . .

○ have the ability to concentrate on specific physical and mental tasks for long periods of time
○ have good manual dexterity
○ have knowledge of artistic techniques
○ have a love of art
○ be willing to continuously learn about new conservation techniques throughout your career

Associate conservators average $45,000 annually. Conservation technicians earn starting salaries of $18,000 to $21,000 per year. The U.S. Department of Labor reports that conservators and museum technicians earned from $20,600 to $61,270 or more in 2006.

EXPLORING

○ Learn art and craft techniques, such as furniture or wood refinishing, oil painting, plastering, and embroidery.
○ Visit museums and ask if they offer behind-the-scenes tours that might include talking to conservators.

Outlook

Employment of conservators and conservation technicians will grow about as fast as average, according to the U.S. Department of Labor. Competition for these desirable positions, however, will be strong.

People will always be interested in cultural artifacts, so there will continue to be a need for qualified conservation workers. Museums often depend on government funds and grants, which can be uncertain. Private conservation companies and for-profit companies may offer more opportunities in the future for conservation workers than museums and nonprofit organizations.

FOR MORE INFO

For information on the conservation field and conservation training, contact
The American Institute for Conservation of Historic and Artistic Works
1156 15th Street NW, Suite 320
Washington, DC 20005-1714
Tel: 202-452-9545
E-mail: info@aic-faic.org
http://aic.stanford.edu

For information on conservation opportunities in Canada, contact
Canadian Conservation Institute
1030 Innes Road
Ottawa, ON K1A 0M5 Canada
Tel: 613-998-3721
http://www.cci-icc.gc.ca

Creative Arts Therapists

What Creative Arts Therapists Do

Creative arts therapists help rehabilitate people with mental, physical, and emotional disabilities. They usually work as part of a health care team of physicians, nurses, psychiatrists, psychologists, and social workers. Therapists work in hospitals, schools, rehabilitation centers, shelters for battered women, substance abuse programs, hospices, and correctional facilities. Some therapists have their own private practices.

The goal of creative arts therapists is to improve their patients physically, mentally, and emotionally. Before they begin any treatment, they meet with a team of other health care professionals. After they determine the strength, limitations, and interests of a patient, they create a special program for him or her. Creative arts therapists continue to meet with the other health care workers during the course of the program. They change the program

Words to Learn

acting out uncontrolled, often aggressive behavior

impulsive disorder any disorder in which a person acts on impulse without thinking about the consequences of the action

portfolio a collection of artwork that shows examples of an artist's skills and techniques

psychotherapy the treatment of mental disorders by psychological, rather than physical, means

according to the patient's progress. How these goals are reached depends on the unique specialty of the therapist.

There are many types of creative arts therapists. *Music therapists* use music lessons and activities to improve a patient's self-confidence. Playing a musical instrument can help a patient's depression and improve physical dexterity. *Art therapists* teach patients to express their thoughts, feelings, and anxieties through sketching, drawing, painting, or sculpting. *Dance and movement therapists* teach dance exercises to help improve the physical, mental, and emotional health of patients. *Drama therapists* use role-playing, pantomime (the telling of a story by the use of expressive body or facial movements), puppetry, improvisation, and performance to increase self-confidence and help patients express themselves. *Poetry therapists* and *bibliotherapists* teach patients to write and speak about their experiences and feelings, which is a powerful way to get rid of anxiety, depression, and fear.

EXPLORING

○ Take music, art, drama, or dance lessons offered in your community. Many community programs offer arts classes to those with disabilities. You might be able to find classes where you can learn along with students that have developmental or physical disabilities.

○ Volunteer at a hospital, clinic, nursing home, or health care facility to learn about working with people who have disabilities. You might be able to assist in creative therapy sessions.

○ You can get experience by working at a summer camp for children with disabilities.

Education and Training

If you plan to become a creative arts therapist, you should begin studying the arts as early as possible. Classes in art, art history, drama, music, and writing will give you important background skills for whichever arts field interests you. You should also take an introductory class in psychology. Communication classes will give you an understanding of the various ways people communicate, both verbally and nonverbally.

How It All Began

Art therapy is based on the idea that people who can't discuss their problems can use other ways to express themselves. In the early 1900s, psychiatrists began to look more closely at their patients' artwork.

In the 1930s, art educators discovered that children often expressed their thoughts better with pictures and role-playing than they did through speaking. Children often don't know the words to explain how they feel, or how to make their needs known to adults. Researchers began to look into art as a treatment for children who were abused, neglected, ill, or had other physical or emotional disabilities.

During and after World War II, the Department of Veterans Affairs (VA) developed art, music, and dance activities for patients in VA hospitals. These activities had a dramatic effect on the physical and mental well-being of the World War II veterans. Creative arts therapists began to use the same activities to treat and rehabilitate patients in other health care settings.

A bachelor's degree is the minimum requirement to become a creative arts therapist. Usually a creative arts therapist earns an undergraduate degree in art, music, or drama and then continues in a master's program. Many colleges and universities offer degrees in specific creative arts therapy fields. A master's degree in education, counseling, or a related field is acceptable. Upon completion of the master's degree, creative arts therapists can apply for certification in their specialty. Creative arts therapists who work in public schools must also be licensed by their state's department of education.

Earnings

Starting salaries for creative arts therapists generally range between $25,000 and $35,000. Therapists with experience usually earn about $45,000. Those creative arts therapists who have administrative or managerial duties can earn from $50,000 to $100,000 a year.

Outlook

Creative arts therapy programs are growing rapidly. Many new positions are being created each year for trained workers. Job openings in nursing homes will increase as the elderly population continues to grow. There will also be jobs in managed care facilities, chronic pain clinics, and cancer care facilities. The outlook for creative arts therapists will continue to brighten as more people become aware of the need to help people with disabilities.

FOR MORE INFO

For information on educational programs and careers, contact

American Art Therapy Association
5999 Stevenson Avenue
Alexandria, VA 22304-3304
Tel: 888-290-0878
E-mail: info@arttherapy.org
http://www.arttherapy.org

American Dance Therapy Association
2000 Century Plaza, Suite 108
10632 Little Patuxent Parkway
Columbia, MD 21044-6258
Tel: 410-997-4040
E-mail: info@adta.org
http://www.adta.org

American Music Therapy Association
8455 Colesville Road, Suite 1000
Silver Spring, MD 20910-3392
Tel: 301-589-3300
E-mail: info@musictherapy.org
http://www.musictherapy.org

National Association for Drama Therapy
15 Post Side Lane
Pittsford, NY 14534-9410
Tel: 585-381-5618
E-mail: answers@nadt.org
http://www.nadt.org

National Association for Poetry Therapy
c/o Center for Education, Training & Holistic Approaches
777 East Atlantic Avenue, #243
Delray Beach, FL 33483-5360
Tel: 866-844-6278
http://www.poetrytherapy.org

For an overview of the various types of art therapy, visit the NCATA's Web site

National Coalition of Creative Arts Therapies Associations (NCATA)
8455 Colesville Road, Suite 1000
Silver Spring, MD 20910-3392
http://www.nccata.org

Fashion Designers

What Fashion Designers Do

Fashion designers design clothing. A small number of designers in New York Paris, Milan, London, and other cities decide on new colors and create styles that set fashion trends. Most designers, however, work for textile, apparel, and pattern manufacturers. Some work for fashion salons, high-fashion department stores, and specialty shops. A few design costumes for the theater and movies.

Designers first figure out what their customers want and need. They do rough sketches and then draw pattern pieces on large sheets of paper. The patterns are laid on the fabric to provide cutting guidelines. Some designers prefer to drape fabric on a dressmaker's dummy. They pin or stitch inexpensive fabric, such as muslin, directly on the dummy. When the fabric pieces are removed from the dummy, they are used to make paper patterns.

Once the final pieces are cut and sewn, designers fit them on a model. This sample garment is shown to buyers, and alterations are made as needed. In small shops, designers work on all phases of fashion production. In larger companies, designers design and draw the original style, while other steps are left to *pattern makers*, *graders* (who draw the paper patterns in various sizes), and *sewers*.

Fashion Fundamentals

○ **harmony** all parts of a fashion design should work together

○ **proportion** all parts of an outfit should relate to one another in size, length, and bulk

○ **emphasis** a garment should have one feature that attracts the eye

○ **balance** a garment should have equal interest in all directions from the main center of interest

A student in a college fashion design class works on a design. (Mary Heitner, The Image Works)

Fashion designers who work for large firms that mass-produce clothing often create 50 to 150 designs for each season's showings. They work on spring and summer designs during the fall and winter months and on fall and winter clothing during the summer months. Some designers work for a few individual

What Costume Designers Do

Costume designers create, coordinate, and organize the costumes for theater, television, and movies. They also create costumes for figure skaters, ballroom dancers, and other performers.

Costume designers read scripts and then plan costumes for each character. If the story takes place in the past, designers do research to make certain that the clothing styles are correct for the time period.

Costume designers make color sketches of the outfits and accessories for each character. They decide whether to rent, purchase, or sew the costumes, depending on the show's budget. They shop for clothing and accessories, fabrics, and sewing supplies. They supervise the assistants who do the sewing work.

EXPLORING

○ Practice your sewing skills. Start by using commercial patterns available at fabric stores. Frequent sewing will make you familiar with flat patterns and the various steps in clothing construction.

○ Art and design courses will help you work on your sketching and drawing ability, and develop your color sense.

○ Keep a sketchbook of fashion ideas. Collect fabric swatches and match them to the fashions you have drawn.

○ Visit fabric stores often and look at the materials available, including fabrics, buttons, threads, ribbons, and other notions.

clients. In fact, many designers start this way. As their reputation and number of clients grows, so does their business, until they are creating a full set of designs for each new season.

Education and Training

Designers must be creative, have the ability to draw, and work well with their hands. Math skills are important for developing the skills of making a flat pattern into a shaped garment, sizing patterns, and measuring yardage.

The best way to become a fashion designer is to complete a two- or three-year program in design from a fashion school. Some colleges offer a four-year degree in fine arts with a major in fashion design.

Earnings

Fashion designers earned average annual salaries of $62,610 in 2006, according to the U.S. Department of Labor. Salaries ranged from less than $30,000 to more than $117,120. A few highly skilled and well-known designers in top firms have annual incomes of more than $150,000. Top fashion designers who have successful lines of clothing can earn bonuses that bring their annual incomes into the millions of dollars, but there are few designers in this category.

Outlook

It is estimated that there are approximately 17,000 designers and assistant designers in the United States and that they represent less than 1 percent of all garment industry employees. Good designers always will be needed, although not in great numbers. According to the U.S. Department of Labor, employment of designers is expected to grow more slowly than the average. However, increasing populations and growing personal incomes should increase the demand for fashion designers.

FOR MORE INFO

For industry information, contact
Council of Fashion Designers of America
1412 Broadway, Suite 2006
New York, NY 10018-9250
http://www.cfda.com

For eductational information, contact
Fashion Institute of Technology
Seventh Avenue at 27th Street
New York, NY 10001-5992
Tel: 212-217-7999
http://www.fitnyc.edu

For a list of accredited schools, contact
National Association of Schools of Art and Design
11250 Roger Bacon Drive, Suite 21
Reston, VA 20190-5248
Tel: 703-437-0700
E-mail: info@arts-accredit.org
http://nasad.arts-accredit.org

Fashion Illustrators and Photographers

What Fashion Illustrators and Photographers Do

Fashion illustrators and photographers work in a glamorized, intense environment. The focus of their art is styles of clothing. They work for advertising agencies, the news media, catalog houses, and fashion magazines.

Fashion illustrators create illustrations that appear in print and electronic formats. Illustrations are used to advertise new fashions, promote models, and popularize certain designers. Some illustrators provide artwork to accompany editorial pieces in magazines such as *Glamour, Redbook,* and *Seventeen* and newspapers such as *Women's Wear Daily.* Catalog companies also employ illustrators to provide the artwork that sells their merchandise through print or online publications.

Fashion illustrators work with fashion designers, editors, and models. They make sketches from designers' notes or they may sketch live models during runway shows or other fashion presentations. They use pencils, pen and ink, charcoal, paint, airbrush, or a combination of media to create their work. In addition to working with pens and paper, fashion

Early Fashion Illustration?

Illustration featured prominently in the ancient civilizations of Mesopotamia, Egypt, and later Greek and Roman civilizations. Drawings of figures conveying power or ideas have also been found among ancient Assyrian, Babylonian, Egyptian, and Chinese societies. Modern illustration began during the Renaissance of the 15th and 16th centuries, with the work of Leonardo da Vinci, Andreas Vesalius, and Michelangelo Buonarotti.

illustrators also need to be able to work with computer programs designed to manipulate their artwork.

The advertising industry is probably the largest employer of fashion photographers. These artists create the pictures that sell clothing, cosmetics, shoes, accessories, and beauty products. Fashion photographers' tools include cameras, film, filters, lenses, tripods, and lighting equipment. Those who do their own developing have darkroom facilities. Fashion photographers sometimes are in charge of choosing a location for a shoot, such as a beach or a train station, or they may construct a studio set. They work with a team of people, including designers, editors, models, photo stylists, hair stylists, and makeup artists. The team works together to create shots that make the clothes and the models look good. Catalog shots tend to be straightforward, showing as much detail in the clothing as possible. Photographs for fashion magazines and advertising are often more creative, conveying a particular mood and emphasizing glamour.

The fashion world is fast paced and competitive. The hours can be long, and there is pressure to produce good work under tight deadlines. Illustrators and photographers may have to face rejection of their work when they

A college fashion illustration class draws a live model. (Mary Heitner, The Image Works)

EXPLORING

○ Explore your interest in the fashion field by reading fashion magazines that will keep you up to date on fashion trends and styles in advertising, photography, and art.

○ Take drawing and photography classes offered by your school or a community center.

○ Join your school's yearbook, newspaper, or literary magazine. These publications often include student illustrations and photographs along with text.

○ Apply for a part-time job at an art supply, photography, or retail clothing store.

Try It Yourself

The best way to see if you have what it takes to become a fashion illustrator is to start drawing. Use the following Web site to practice drawing basic modeling figures and read tips about using other materials such as glue, pens, and mounting boards.

Fashion Drawing Tutorial Tips
http://www.fashion-era.com/drawing_fashion.htm

are starting out until they can earn a reputation and develop a style that is in demand.

Education and Training

There are no formal education requirements for fashion illustrators or photographers. Many high schools offer photography classes, and most offer art courses. For both photographers and illustrators, the best education is practice.

As you continue to practice your art, you will begin to build a portfolio of your work, or a collection of the best of your sketches or photos. There are some vocational or fashion schools that offer classes in fashion illustration. These classes not only teach you art technique but also teach you how to assemble and present your portfolio. Photography programs are widely available from the associate's degree level to the bachelor's degree level. Photographers can apprentice themselves to established photographers to learn about photographic techniques and the fashion world, and also to develop contacts in the industry.

Earnings

The U.S. Department of Labor reports that salaried fine artists, including illustrators, had earnings that ranged from less than

$18,350 to $79,390 or more in 2006. Illustrators employed in advertising and related services had mean annual incomes of $44,520. Photographers employed in all industries had median annual earnings of $26,170 in 2006. Salaries ranged from less than $15,540 to $56,640 or more annually.

Earning potential for both fashion illustrators and fashion photographers depends on where their work is published. A large fashion magazine is able to pay more for an illustration or photograph than a small publisher. Illustrators and photographers who build a strong portfolio of published work and work

FOR MORE INFO

For information on this school, contact
Fashion Institute of Technology
Seventh Avenue at 27th Street
New York, NY 10001-5992
Tel: 212-217-7999
http://www.fitnyc.edu

For a list of accredited schools, contact
National Association of Schools of Art and Design
11250 Roger Bacon Drive, Suite 21
Reston, VA 20190-5248
Tel: 703-437-0700
E-mail: info@arts-accredit.org
http://nasad.arts-accredit.org

This organization offers various services for its members.
Professional Photographers of America
229 Peachtree Street NE, Suite 2200
Atlanta, GA 30303-1608
Tel: 800-786-6277
http://www.ppa.com

For career information, contact
Society of Illustrators
128 East 63rd Street
New York, NY 10021-7303
Tel: 212-838-2560
E-mail: info@societyillustrators.org
http://www.societyillustrators.org

This Web site allows you to browse through galleries of hundreds of established fashion photographers.
FashionBook.com
http://www.fashionbook.com

Visit this site for more career advice.
Fashion Net: How to Become a Fashion Photographer
http://www.fashion.net/howto/photography

Visit this site to view several examples of fashion sketches.
Metrofashion
http://www.metrofashion.com/sketches.html

for more prestigious clients can make hundreds of thousands of dollars a year.

Outlook

Employment for visual artists and photographers is expected to grow as fast as the average over the next several years. For illustrators and photographers specifically working in fashion, employment will likely be dependent on the economic health of advertising firms, magazines, newspapers, and fashion houses and other businesses involved in fashion. The outlook for these businesses currently looks strong. In addition, numerous outlets for fashion, such as e-zines and retail Web sites, will create a need for illustrators and photographers. Competition for jobs, however, will be keen, since these positions are highly attractive to people with artistic ability. The growing popularity of digital cameras and computer art programs presents new options for artists to explore.

Graphic Designers

What Graphic Designers Do

Graphic designers plan how to arrange artwork and lettering for books, magazines, television programs, advertisements, product packaging, and Web sites.

Graphic designers receive materials for their assignments from editors and writers, illustrators, and photographers. They might receive special instructions from art directors or publishers. They have to consider the medium—print, computer, or film—and the audience. They decide on a central point of focus, such as the title of a magazine article or the name of a product on a package. They size the lettering; choose and size the artwork, whether it's an illustration, photograph, or logo; and choose colors. Designers for already existing magazines, newspapers, and other periodicals usually have to follow a regular format that makes every issue look consistent. Some graphic designers create logos for companies or draw charts and graphs.

Graphic design is a process. For example, when designing a cover for a book, designers make two or three rough designs for the client to look at. The client might choose one of the designs immediately, or ask a designer to change the type size, color, or another element. Designers rework their pieces until their clients are satisfied. Then they prepare the final piece for print or film.

Type Choices

lower case	SMALL CAPS
UPPER CASE	underline
roman	shadow
bold	outline
italic	serif
bold italic	sans serif

EXPLORING

○ Take as many art and design courses as you can. If your school does not offer them, you might be able to find them offered at community centers or art schools.

○ Learn different software programs for page layout and illustration. Design your own publications.

○ Participate in school and community projects that call for design talents. These might include building sets for plays, setting up exhibits, planning seasonal and holiday displays, and preparing concert programs and other printed materials.

○ Work on the layout of your school newspaper or yearbook.

Each medium is different. Graphic designers in film and television design the credits and other type that appears on screen. They also work on animated graphics, maps, and charts. In product packaging, designers must be able to visualize a three-dimensional object that will be printed from a flat piece of artwork. Web sites require a different layout style than magazine pages. Graphic designers usually specialize in one of these media.

Graphic designers are employed by design studios, advertising firms, publishing companies, printers, television studios, manufacturing firms, and retail stores. Many designers work independently as freelancers. All designers today do their work on computers, using illustration, photo manipulation, scanning, and page layout software.

Education and Training

Classes in mathematics, art, and computer science are a good foundation for this field. Most employers prefer to hire people who have had formal art education. The best preparation after high school is a four-year art school program that leads to a bachelor of fine arts degree. There are art schools that offer a specialty in graphic design or advertising design. Some graphic designers receive their training at vocational schools that teach the required technical skills for a beginning job. Since computer skills are increasingly important, some formal education in computer graphics is highly recommended.

How Freelancers Find Clients

Many graphic designers work as freelancers. It can be difficult, especially when starting out, to find new clients. Freelancers have to spend a lot of time marketing their talents and finding assignments. Here are some methods they use.

○ Friends may have contacts in different businesses. They might be able to arrange an interview with a potential client.

○ Professional organizations hold meetings and advertise available jobs for their members.

○ Demonstrations and classes can offer opportunities to meet other designers and clients.

○ Freelancers sometimes design and print a brochure that demonstrates their talent and then send it to potential clients.

○ Freelancers can also make contacts by attending meetings, lectures, or gatherings for causes that interest them. For example, a graphic designer might attend a food-related convention and meet a restaurant owner who needs menu designs.

Designers often start out as production artists or computer graphic technicians. Some even work as art teachers before becoming full-time designers.

Earnings

Graphic designers earn as little as $20,000 to more than $110,000 a year, depending on the nature of their work and their employers. Entry-level graphic designers earned approximately $24,000 in 2006, according to the U.S. Department of Labor. Salaried designers who advance to the position of design

FOR MORE INFO

For more information about careers in graphic design, contact

American Institute of Graphic Arts
164 Fifth Avenue
New York, NY 10010-5901
Tel: 212-807-1990
http://www.aiga.org

For a list of accredited schools, contact

National Association of Schools of Art and Design
11250 Roger Bacon Drive, Suite 21
Reston, VA 20190-5248
Tel: 703-437-0700
E-mail: info@arts-accredit.org
http://nasad.arts-accredit.org

For information on publication design, contact

Society of Publication Designers
17 East 47th Street, 6th Floor
New York, NY 10017-1920
Tel: 212-223-3332
E-mail: mail@spd.org
http://www.spd.org

manager or design director earn about $75,000 a year. The owner of a consulting firm can make $130,000 or more.

Outlook

Employment for graphic designers is expected to grow about as fast as the average, according to the U.S. Department of Labor. Employment should be especially strong for those involved with computer graphics and animation.

Because the design field appeals to many talented individuals, competition is expected to be strong in all areas. Beginners and designers with only average talent or without formal education and skills may have some difficulty finding jobs.

Illustrators

What Illustrators Do

Illustrators create artwork with a variety of media—pencil, pen and ink, pastels, paints (oil, acrylic, watercolor), airbrush, collage, and computer programs. Illustrations appear in books, magazines, newspapers, signs and billboards, packaging, Web sites, computer programs, greeting cards, calendars, stationery, and direct mail.

Illustrators often work as part of a creative team, which includes graphic designers, photographers, and those who draw lettering, or *calligraphers*. Most illustrators are self-employed, but some work in advertising agencies, design firms, commercial art firms, or printing and publishing companies. They are also employed in the motion picture and television industries, retail stores, catalog companies, and public relations firms.

Some illustrators specialize. *Medical illustrators*, for example, make drawings, paintings, and three-dimensional models of medical procedures and specimens. Their work appears in textbooks, advertisements, medical journals, video, and films. *Fashion illustrators* work for advertising agencies, newspapers, catalog houses, and fashion magazines. They attend fashion shows and work closely with fashion designers to make sure clothing colors and styles are represented accurately. *Natural science illustrators* create illustrations of plants and wildlife. They often work at museums such as the Smithsonian Institution. *Children's book illustrators* specialize in creating artwork for books and other publications for young people.

Most illustrators become known for their particular style and medium (paint, pen and ink, pastel, pencil, and collage to name

Profile: Maxfield Parrish (1870–1966)

Maxfield Parrish was an American illustrator and painter known for his use of color and his decorative, humorous pictures.

Parrish illustrated Eugene Field's *Poems of Childhood,* Kenneth Grahame's *Golden Age,* and other books. He did advertisements, illustrations, and covers for such magazines as *Harper's Weekly.* Among his murals are *Pied Piper* in the Sheraton-Palace Hotel in San Francisco and *Old King Cole* in the St. Regis Hotel in New York City.

Parrish was born in Philadelphia and attended Haverford College and the Pennsylvania Academy of Fine Arts. He also studied with illustrator, Howard Pyle.

To learn more about Maxfield Parrish, visit the following Web site: http://www.bpib.com/illustrat/parrish.htm

a few). Until they become well known, they spend a great deal of time showing their portfolio to clients.

Education and Training

To become an illustrator, you must develop your artistic and creative abilities. Take art classes and learn computer illustration programs as well.

Talent is perhaps more important to an illustrator's success than education or training. Education, however, will teach you about new techniques and media, and help you build your portfolio. Whether you plan to look for full-time employment or freelance assignments, you will need a portfolio that contains samples of your best work. Employers are especially interested in work that has been published or printed. To find a salaried position as an illustrator, you will need at least a high school diploma and preferably an associate's degree in commercial art or fine art. Most medical illustrators have master's degrees from graduate programs in medical illustration. There are five of these programs in the United States and Canada, and each accepts only a small number of students each year.

Earnings

The pay for illustrations can be as little as a byline (a line under the title that gives your name). In the beginning of your career a byline may be worthwhile so that many people can become familiar with your work. Experienced illustrators can earn several thousand dollars for a single work. Average earnings for full-time visual artists ranged from $18,350 to $79,390 or more a year in 2006, according to the U.S. Department of Labor. Medical illustrators

EXPLORING

○ Take art classes that help you experiment with different media.
○ Keep a sketch diary, in which you draw every day. Artistic talent is important, but won't get you very far if you don't practice and work at your art.
○ Submit artwork for your school newspaper, yearbook, or literary publication.
○ Join an art club at your school or community center.
○ Make posters for school and community events.

Learn More About It

Fleishman, Michael. *Starting Your Career as a Freelance Illustrator or Graphic Designer.* New York: Allworth Press, 2001.

Hodges, Elaine R. S. (ed.) *The Guild Handbook of Scientific Illustration.* 2d ed. Hoboken, N.J.: John Wiley & Sons, 2003.

Pope, Alice.(ed.) 2007 *Children's Writer's & Illustrator's Market.* 19th ed. Cincinnati, Ohio: Writers Digest Books, 2006.

Reed, Walt. *The Illustrator in America, 1860–2000.* 3d ed. New York: Watson-Guptill Publications, 2001.

Slade, Catharine. *The Encyclopedia of Illustration Techniques.* Philadelphia: Running Press, 1997.

start at around $35,000 per year. The average pay for an experienced medical illustrator ranges from $45,000 to $75,000 a year.

Outlook

Employment of illustrators is expected to grow about as fast as the average, according to the U.S. Department of Labor. The continuing growth of the Internet should provide more opportunities for illustrators.

The field of medical illustration is small, but the field of medicine and science in general is always growing, and medical illustrators will be needed to depict new techniques, procedures, and discoveries.

FOR MORE INFO

For information on educational and career opportunities for medical illustrators, contact
Association of Medical Illustrators
810 East 10th Street
Lawrence, KS 66044-3018
Tel: 866-393-4264
E-mail: hq@ami.org
http://www.ami.org

This organization promotes and protects the financial interests of artists.
Graphic Artists Guild
32 Broadway, Suite 1114
New York, NY 10004-1612
Tel: 212-791-3400
http://www.gag.org

For information on membership, contact
Guild of Natural Science Illustrators
PO Box 652
Ben Franklin Station

Washington, DC 20044-0652
Tel: 301-309-1514
E-mail: gnsihome@his.com
http://www.gnsi.org

For career information, contact
Society of Children's Book Writers and Illustrators
8271 Beverly Boulevard
Los Angeles, CA 90048-4515
Tel: 323-782-1010
E-mail: scbwi@scbwi.org
http://www.scbwi.org

For career information, contact
Society of Illustrators
128 East 63rd Street
New York, NY 10021-7303
Tel: 212-838-2560
E-mail: info@societyillustrators.org
http://www.societyillustrators.org

Interior Designers and Decorators

What Interior Designers and Decorators Do

Interior designers and decorators plan and design the rooms of houses, offices, hotels, restaurants, factories, theaters, stores, and other buildings. They help their customers select equipment and fixtures. They plan the arrangement of furniture, draperies, floor coverings, wallpaper, paint, and other decorations. They coordinate an entire decorating project from beginning to end.

Interior designers begin by deciding how the space will be used. Is it living or working space? How many people will occupy the space? What are the traffic patterns? They also think about what their customers want, as well as how much these customers can spend. Interior designers often work closely with architects, painters, carpenters, carpet layers, drapery hangers, and floor covering specialists. Designers must be familiar with building and zoning laws that affect the project they're working on.

Once designers have seen the space that they will be decorating, they make sketches or models of their plans. They estimate how much the materials and the

Questions Interior Designers Ask

Style: Will the style be traditional or contemporary? Formal or informal? Lively or subdued?

Scale: Is the furniture in scale with the size of the room and the sizes of other furnishings?

Color: Do selected colors set the desired mood? Do they work well with the room's size and shape?

Pattern: Will fabrics, carpeting, and wallpaper be a solid color, or will they have a pattern?

Arrangement: Is furniture grouped and the room arranged so that people can move around freely?

Lighting: Does the lighting go with the room's style and colors?

EXPLORING

○ Study different styles of furniture, window treatments, and floor coverings.

○ Read decorating magazines, such as *House Beautiful* or *Architectural Digest.* Cut out pictures and keep a scrapbook of interior designs you like.

○ Ask your parents if you can redecorate your own room or help with other decorating projects at home. Choose paint colors, curtain fabric, and wall decorations. Plan several ways to arrange the furniture.

○ Visit fabric stores and look at fabrics in the upholstery and drapery departments. There are fabric stores that carry only fabrics for interior decorating. Try to find colors, patterns, and textures that might go together.

work will cost and present their findings to their clients. If the clients approve the plans, the designers buy materials, such as drapery and upholstery fabrics, furniture, paint, and wallpaper. Then they work with various craft specialists to make sure that the plans are carried out.

Some designers and decorators specialize in a specific area of interior design, such as furniture, carpeting, or artwork. Others specialize in particular environments, such as offices, hospitals, houses, or restaurants. Still others specialize in restoring old buildings.

Education and Training

If you're thinking about a career as an interior designer or decorator, study history, art history, architectural drawing and drafting, and fine arts.

Most interior designers earn a two- or three-year certificate or diploma from an interior design school or a degree from a college or university. Advanced courses at design schools and universities will include furniture design, codes and standards of design, lighting and electrical equipment, computer-aided design, and classes that focus on the types of materials used, such as fibers, wood, metals, and plastics. Most architectural firms, department stores, and design firms accept only professionally trained people, even for entry-level positions.

Earnings

Interior designers earned median annual salaries of about $42,260 in 2006, according to the U.S. Department of Labor.

Salaries ranged from $24,270 to $78,760 a year or more. Interior designers working in large urban areas make significantly more than those who work in smaller cities.

Designers and decorators at interior design firms can earn a straight salary, a salary plus a bonus or commission, or a straight commission. Design firms sometimes pay their employees a percentage of the profits as well. Self-employed professionals may charge an hourly fee, a flat fee, or a combination of the two depending on the project.

Outlook

Employment opportunities are expected to be good for interior designers and decorators well into the next decade. Since the services of design

An interior designer (left) instructs a client on how to use computer-aided interior design technology. (Topham, The Image Works)

A New Old Trend in Interior Design

Feng shui, which literally means "wind and water," is an ancient Chinese art and science developed over 5,000 years ago. It has become a new trend in interior design because it is concerned with the proper and beneficial placement of all things, including doors, bedrooms, kitchens, furnishings, and accessories. It is believed that the arrangement of these items can increase harmony, happiness, good relationships, and prosperity.

The principles of feng shui, as applied to interior decorating, include removing clutter, rearranging furniture, and placing beds, desks, and chairs in proper positions. Decorators also use aquariums, water fountains, metal and moving metal, broad leaf plants, earthenware, and other feng shui cures.

For more information on feng shui, visit http://fengshui.about.com.

FOR MORE INFO

For industry trends, career guidance, and other resources, contact
American Society of Interior Designers
608 Massachusetts Avenue NE
Washington, DC 20002-6006
Tel: 202-546-3480
http://www.asid.org

For information on careers and a list of educational programs in interior design, contact
Interior Design Educators Council
7150 Winton Drive, Suite 300
Indianapolis, IN 46268-4398
Tel: 317-328-4437
E-mail: info@idec.org
http://www.idec.org

For information on the industry, contact
International Interior Design Association
222 Merchandise Mart, Suite 567
Chicago, IL 60654-1103
Tel: 888-799-4432
E-mail: iidahq@iida.org
http://www.iida.org

For useful career information, visit the following Web site
Careers in Interior Design
http://www.careersininteriordesign.com

professionals are in many ways a luxury, the job outlook depends on the economy. With the U.S. economy predicted to remain strong, interior designers with formal training and talent should find plenty of career opportunities. Work will continue to be available in interior design firms, department stores, architectural firms, and large corporations.

Jewelers

What Jewelers Do

Jewelers design and make rings, necklaces, earrings, and bracelets. They use metals like gold, silver, and platinum and a variety of precious and semiprecious gems, such as diamonds, emeralds, and rubies. Some specialize in cutting and shaping gemstones, and others specialize in setting the gems. Some jewelers design and make the precious metal setting. Most jewelers also make repairs, resize rings, reset stones, and refashion old jewelry.

Jewelers work at a tool bench, with easy access to a wide variety of electric and hand tools. Most tools are small for detailed, precise work. Jewelers use awls, pliers, hammers, drills, soldering irons, wire cutters, grinders, polishers, and other tools. They wear goggles and take other safety precautions to protect their hands and to keep from breathing harmful chemicals.

Jewelers need a great deal of patience and concentration for their painstaking work. They must have excellent eye-hand coordination. Those who make their own designs need artistic talent and the ability to visualize and work in three dimensions.

Some jewelers work for manufacturing plants, designing the models and tools needed to mass-produce costume jewelry. Others work in jewelry stores owned by a businessperson

Did You Know?

In 2004, about 42,000 jewelers were employed in the United States, and about 40 percent of them were self-employed. Most self-employed jewelers own their own stores or repair shops or specialize in designing and creating custom jewelry. Of all salaried jewelers, 30 percent worked in retail stores and 20 percent were employed in manufacturing plants, according to the U.S. Department of Labor.

EXPLORING

○ Hobbies such as model making, metalworking, and sculpture will help you become familiar with metals, adhesives, and the tools jewelers use.

○ Participate in arts and crafts activities and take classes in your school or community. Art stores and museums may also offer classes.

○ Visit museums and fine jewelry stores to see collections of jewelry.

○ Visit art fairs and craft shows where jewelers exhibit and sell their products.

○ Most art stores carry jewelry-making supplies. You can learn some basic techniques on your own, such as stringing beads and attaching findings like necklace clasps or earring wires.

who is not a jeweler, and still others own and manage their own shops. These independent jewelers often sell fine merchandise, such as silverware, china, and glassware, in addition to selling and repairing jewelry and watches.

Education and Training

You need at least a high school education to become a jeweler. Courses in art, design, chemistry, and metalwork are helpful. Many trade schools and community colleges offer programs in jewelry making and repair. Classes cover basic jewelry-making skills, use of tools, stone polishing, and gem identification. These programs take from 6 to 36 months to complete. Many jewelers learn through informal on-the-job training or by completing a two-year apprenticeship program with an experienced

Gems Through History

Humanity has known about gemstones for 7,000 years. Amethyst, amber, garnet, jade, lapis lazuli, emerald, and turquoise were some of the first gemstones used, and they were usually status symbols for royalty. All throughout history and up to modern times, gems have been used as amulets and talismans to ward off evil, promote health, or bring travelers safely home. Early on, certain gemstones became associated with signs of the zodiac and eventually became known as birthstones. Today, gemstones have lost much of their symbolic value and are collected as investments.

To Be a Successful Jeweler, You Should . . .

○ have superior hand-eye coordination

○ be good at basic mechanical skills such as filing, sawing, and drilling

○ be creative and artistic

○ have a strong understanding of metals and their properties

○ have good people skills

○ have a knowledge of merchandising and business management and practices if you own your own business

jeweler or in a jewelry manufacturing plant. Most apprentices must pass written, oral, and practical tests at the end of the program.

Earnings

Jewelers earned annual salaries of $29,750 in 2006, according to the U.S. Department of Labor. Salaries ranged from less than $17,760 to $54,940 or more. Jewelers and other workers in manufacturing earned mean salaries of $29,320, with jewelers earning significantly more than those in unskilled or semiskilled positions. Retail store owners and jewelry artists and designers can earn between $30,000 and $100,000 or more yearly.

Outlook

Employment of jewelers is expected to decline, according to the U.S. Department of Labor. Despite this prediction, jewelers and jewelry repairers will continue to be needed to replace those workers who leave the workforce or move to new positions. Since jewelry sales are increasing at rates that exceed the number of new jewelers entering the profession, employers are finding it difficult to find skilled employees.

FOR MORE INFO

For answers to frequently asked questions about jewelry, visit the society's Web site
American Gem Society
8881 West Sahara Avenue
Las Vegas, NV 89117-5865
Tel: 866-805-6500
http://www.americangemsociety.org

For information on designer jewelry, contact
American Jewelry Design Council
760 Market Street, Suite 900
San Francisco, CA 94102-2304
http://www.ajdc.org

For an information packet, contact
Gemological Institute of America
The Robert Mouawad Campus
5345 Armada Drive
Carlsbad, CA 92008-4602
http://www.gia.edu

For a school directory and a copy of Careers in the Jewelry Industry, *contact*
Jewelers of America
52 Vanderbilt Avenue, 19th Floor
New York, NY 10017-3827
Tel: 800-223-0673
E-mail: info@jewelers.org
http://www.jewelers.org

For career and education information, contact
Manufacturing Jewelers and Suppliers of America
45 Royal Little Drive
Providence, RI 02904-1861
Tel: 800-444-6572
E-mail: info@mjsa.org
http://www.mjsa.org

Makeup Artists

What Makeup Artists Do

Makeup artists design and apply makeup for stage and screen actors. They read scripts and meet with directors, producers, and technicians. They create special effects ranging from scars and prosthetics to radio-controlled mechanical body parts. Sometimes makeup artists apply "clean" (natural-looking) makeup and eliminate or apply wrinkles, tattoos, or scars. When they design makeup, makeup artists must consider the age of the characters, the setting and period of the film or play, and the lighting effects that will be used. Historical productions require considerable research to design hair, makeup, and fashion styles of a particular era. Makeup artists also may work on hair, but in many states locally licensed cosmetologists must be brought in for hair cutting, coloring, and perms.

Once the actors have been made up, makeup artists play an important role during production as well. They watch the monitors constantly during filming to make sure the makeup is just right. They reapply or adjust the actors' makeup as needed throughout filming or between scenes. They help the actors remove the makeup at the end of the day. Makeup artists must be able to spot any makeup problems before a scene is filmed.

Profile: Rick Baker (1950–   )

In 1981, when the Academy Awards introduced the Best Makeup category, Rick Baker received the first Oscar for *An American Werewolf in London.* He won his second Oscar for designing Sasquatch Harry in *Harry and the Hendersons* (1987) and his third Oscar for designing and creating the Bela Lugosi makeup for Martin Landau in *Ed Wood* (1994). He won again for *The Nutty Professor* (1996), *Men in Black* (1997), and *Dr. Seuss' How the Grinch Stole Christmas* (2000).

Baker was a fan of horror movies as a child. He experimented with movie makeup effects at a young age and later assisted the famous makeup artist Dick Smith. Rick Baker is considered one of the best makeup artists in the field.

EXPLORING

○ Read publications about the field, such as *Make-Up Artist Magazine* (http://www.makeupmag.com).

○ Volunteer to do makeup for school productions. Make sure to take pictures of your work.

○ Look for opportunities to volunteer your help to local theaters. The summer months will offer the most opportunities. Small community theaters will pay little or nothing, but they may allow you the best chance to explore makeup artistry.

Most makeup artists are self-employed and work on a freelance basis. When they are not working on a film, they might work for television or video projects, commercials, and industrial films to supplement their film work. Makeup artists for the theater may be employed full time by a theater, or they may be freelancers. Makeup artists also work for photographers who do fashion photography.

Education and Training

Most makeup artists have bachelor's or master's degrees in theater, art history, photography, fashion, or a related subject. To prepare for a career as a makeup artist, take art classes, as well as art history, photography, painting,

To Be a Successful Makeup Artist, You Should . . .

○ have detailed knowledge of the many types of makeup

○ have good research skills in order to learn more about makeup styles from past eras

○ be able get along well with people, some of whom may occasionally be difficult to work with

○ be attentive to detail

○ be creative and inventive when designing and applying makeup

○ be persistent and enthusiastic in order to compete for jobs in this highly competitive industry

drawing, anatomy, sculpting, and even chemistry. Participate in school drama productions and assist with makeup whenever possible.

A makeup artist prepares a model for a fashion show. (Jeff Greenberg, The Image Works)

Cosmetology licenses or certificates from special makeup schools are not required, but they may help, especially when you start out. If you are willing to spend some time working for very little pay, or even for free, you can gain valuable experience assisting an experienced, established makeup artist. There are also some highly regarded schools for makeup artists, such as the Joe Blasco Professional Make-Up Artist Training Centers.

Earnings

Makeup artists usually earn a daily rate for their services. This rate varies depending on the budget and size of the production and the experience and reputation of the makeup artist. Day rates can range from $50 for a small theater production, to $300 to $1,000 for experienced makeup artists working on Broadway or feature films. The U.S. Department of Labor reports that theatrical and performance makeup artists had median annual salaries of $31,820 in 2006. Salaries ranged from less than $14,500 to more than $70,750. Work is rarely steady. Most makeup artists work long hours for several weeks and then may be without work for a period.

Outlook

The outlook for makeup artists is good. Many new jobs will become available as the film and television industries continue to grow. Increased use of special effects will require makeup artists with special talent and training. The future for work in theaters is less predictable, but there does appear to be a revived interest in Broadway. This interest could result in better business for traveling productions and regional theaters. On the whole, opportunities for makeup artists are expected to increase.

FOR MORE INFO

To order a copy of or subscription to Make-up Artist Magazine, *contact*
Make-Up Artist Magazine
4018 NE 112th Avenue, Suite D-8
Vancouver, WA 98682-5703
Tel: 800-805-6648
http://www.makeupmag.com

For information about theater jobs and a sample copy of ARTSEARCH, *contact*
Theater Communications Group
520 Eighth Avenue, 24th Floor
New York, NY 10018-4156
Tel: 212-609-5900
Email: tcg@tcg.org
http://www.tcg.org

Merchandise Displayers

What Merchandise Displayers Do

Merchandise displayers design and build displays for windows, showcases, and floors of stores. They are sometimes called *display workers*, *showcase trimmers*, and *window dressers*. Store displays must be artistic and attractive so that customers will want to buy the products.

Some merchandise displayers work in self-service stores. Because there are no salespeople, displays are very important in attracting the customer to buy products. In large retail stores, there may be a large staff of display specialists. Merchandise displayers also prepare product displays for trade shows, exhibitions, conventions, or festivals. They build installations such as booths and exhibits. They also install carpeting, drapes, and other decorations, including flags, banners, and lights, and arrange furniture and other accessories.

Displayers first develop an idea or theme that will highlight the merchandise and attract customers. Display workers use hammers, saws, spray guns, and other hand tools to build displays. They may use carpeting, wallpaper, and special lighting. They build and paint the backdrops and gather all the props they'll need.

A merchandise displayer arranges a mannequin at a women's clothing store. (Margot Granitsas, The Image Works)

EXPLORING

○ You can find lots of opportunities to work on displays at school. Ask your teachers if you can help design and arrange bulletin boards, posters, or displays for special events, such as parents' night and fund-raisers.

○ Participate in groups that are in charge of decorations or publicity for school dances and parties.

○ Help your neighbors arrange items for garage or yard sales.

○ Join your school or community drama group to work on sets, props, and costumes.

○ Take courses offered in your community in art, sculpture, calligraphy, or carpentry.

Finally, they arrange the mannequins and the merchandise and hang printed materials, such as signs, descriptions of the merchandise, and price tags.

Sometimes display workers work in teams where each worker has a specialty, such as sign making, window painting, or carpentry.

Education and Training

Merchandise displayers must have at least a high school education. Courses in art, woodworking, mechanical drawing, and merchandising are useful. Some employers expect their merchandise displayers to have taken college courses in art, fashion merchandising, advertising, or interior decorating.

Art institutes, fashion merchandising schools, and some junior colleges

To Be a Successful Merchandise Displayer, You Should . . .

○ be creative

○ have manual dexterity

○ have mechanical aptitude

○ have strength and physical ability to carry equipment and climb ladders

○ be agile in order to work in close quarters without upsetting the props

○ have strong communication skills

What Do Exhibit Designers Do?

Exhibit designers plan and design displays in museums. They arrange artifacts and objects, or create scenes from other times and places. Along with the objects, they arrange text and other information to explain the display items to viewers.

Exhibit designers meet regularly with curators, educators, and conservators throughout the planning stages. Each exhibit must be educational, and the team plans each exhibition so that it tells a story. They use informative labels, group objects logically, and construct displays that place the objects in proper context.

Exhibit designers must also think about keeping objects safe from harm caused by light, temperature, and movement. Most permanent exhibits are planned four years in advance while temporary exhibits take between 6 and 18 months to prepare.

Museums usually hire exhibit designers who have at least a bachelor's degree in art or design. Courses in museum studies are also helpful. Although design jobs are expected to grow about as fast as the average, the opportunities for exhibit designers may be limited. Many museums rely on grants for funding, so they often face budget problems. Exhibit designers may find more opportunities with private exhibition and design firms. Salaries for exhibit designers range from $21,000 to $76,000 or more. Some larger or better-funded museums, historical societies, and related institutions pay more.

offer courses in merchandise display. Many merchandise displayers receive their training on the job. They may start as sales clerks and learn while assisting window dressers or display workers.

Earnings

Merchandise displayers earned on average $23,820 a year in 2006, according to the U.S. Department of Labor. Beginners earned $15,630 or less and more experienced displayers earned more than $41,000 a year. Freelancers may earn as much as $60,000 a year, but their income depends on their reputation, number of clients, and number of hours they work. Display managers in big-city stores earn more.

Outlook

The employment of display workers is expected to grow at an average rate, according to the U.S. Department of Labor. Retail businesses continue to grow and will need merchandisers to help sell products.

FOR MORE INFO

For industry trends, career guidance, and other resources, contact
American Society of Interior Designers
608 Massachusetts Avenue NE
Washington, DC 20002-6006
Tel: 202-546-3480
http://www.asid.org

For industry information, contact
Institute of Store Planners
25 North Broadway
Tarrytown, NY 10591-3221
Tel: 914-332-0040
E-mail: info@ispo.org
http://www.ispo.org

Photo Stylists

What Photo Stylists Do

Photo stylists work with photographers, art directors, models, and clients to create a visual image. They use props, backgrounds, accessories, food, linens, clothing, costumes, and other set elements to create these images. Much of the work they do is for catalogs and newspaper advertising. Stylists also work on films and television commercials.

Most stylists specialize in fashion, food, hair and makeup, or bridal styling. Some do only prop shopping or location searches. Others prefer to develop a variety of skills so they can find different kinds of photo styling work.

Photo stylists use their imagination, resourcefulness, and artistic skills to set up a shot that will help sell a product. For example, a mail-order clothing company may want a series of ads to sell their winter line of clothing. Photo stylists may decide to design a set outside with a snow background or indoors near a fireplace with holiday decorations in the background. They gather props, such as lamps or table decorations. They rent chairs and couches, then use them to decorate the set where the shoot will take place. Photo stylists hire models to wear the clothing. They may work with other photo stylists and assistants to style the hair and makeup of the models.

Tools of the Trade

Here are some of the things photo stylists might carry with them to photo shoots:

- cloth steamer
- skewers
- toothpicks
- brushes, small and large
- cotton swabs
- tweezers
- utility knife
- glycerine
- oil
- spray bottles
- eye droppers
- blow torch
- mixer
- pastry bags and tips
- safety pins
- needle and thread
- tape

EXPLORING

○ Watch someone prepare a display in a department store window. Many stylists start out as window dressers.

○ Team up with friends and class-mates who are interested in pho-tography or film. Offer to work on setting up shots. A photo shoot can be a good way to learn the elements involved with this career.

○ Work on set design or props for a school or community theater.

○ Join a photography club and learn the basics of taking pictures. This will help you visualize what the photographer sees.

Photo stylists usually have a "bag of tricks" that will solve problems or create certain visual effects. This kit may include everything from duct tape to cotton wadding to a spare salt shaker. Sometimes photo stylists build and design props from scratch. They may have to coordinate the entire pro-duction from finding the location to arranging accommodations. The best photo stylists are versatile and creative enough to come up with ideas and solutions on the spot. If they cannot create or locate something, they have many contacts who can help them out.

Photo stylists must be organized. They must make sure to gather every-thing that they need for a photo shoot and that it is well cared for during the shoot. After the shoot, photo stylists make sure that all borrowed items are returned and that all rentals and other transactions have been recorded.

Education and Training

There is no specific training or schooling to become a photo styl-ist, but there are other ways to prepare for this job. Art classes can help train your eye for design and composition. Experience with building and constructing displays will be of great help. Skill with fabric, such as pressing and steaming clothes, doing minor alterations, and needlework, are important in fashion photo styling. Those interested in hair and makeup styling should take courses in cosmetology. Interior design courses help you arrange room settings. A general knowledge of photography, film, and lighting will help you communicate with photographers.

Styling Specialties

These are some of the specialties in photo styling:

- advertising
- beds and domestics
- bridal
- casting and production
- catalog
- children
- costumes
- editorial
- fashion
- film and video
- jewelry
- lifestyle
- off-figure
- props for food
- props
- set design and interiors
- still life
- tabletop
- visual merchandising
- wardrobe

Most photo stylists enter the field as apprentices to established stylists. Apprentices usually work for two years or more before taking clients on their own.

Earnings

Salaries at production houses can start as low as $8 an hour. Experienced fashion or food stylists can earn as much as $800 a day and more, depending on the stylist's reputation and the budget of the production. On the average, stylists earn around $350 to $500 per day as freelancers. Assistants earn around $150 to $200 a day, according to the Association of Stylists and Coordinators.

Outlook

Good photo stylists are becoming increasingly important to photographers and advertising clients. The employment outlook of photo stylists depends on the health of the advertising, film, and commercial photography industries.

New digital photography and photo enhancement technology may change the role of the photo stylist in the future. Also in the future there may be more educational programs for photo stylists, and this may increase the competition for styling assignments.

FOR MORE INFO

For more information about the work of photo stylists, contact

Association of Stylists and Coordinators
18 East 18th Street, #5E
New York, NY 10003-1933
E-mail: info@stylistsasc.com
http://www.stylistsasc.com

Photographers

What Photographers Do

Photography is both an artistic and technical occupation. There are many variables in the process that a knowledgeable *photographer* can manipulate to produce a clear image or a more abstract work of fine art. First, photographers know how to use cameras and can adjust focus, shutter speeds, aperture, lenses, and filters. They know about the types and speeds of films. Photographers also know about light and shadow, deciding when to use available natural light and when to set up artificial lighting to achieve desired effects.

Some photographers send their film to laboratories, but some develop their own negatives and make their own prints. These processes require knowledge about chemicals such as

Profile: Ansel Adams (1902–1984)

U.S. photographer Ansel Adams was known for his dramatic scenes of the American West and for his contributions to photographic technology. His zone system was a method of controlling film exposure and development to give a range of dark and light tones in black and white prints.

Adams was born in San Francisco, California. He studied music and photography and was a concert pianist until 1930. In 1932 he joined Edward Weston and other photographers in forming Group f/64, which helped establish photography as a fine art. Adams's photos were published in more than 35 books and portfolios. He also wrote many books on photographic techniques, including *The Negative and The Print*.

For more information on Ansel Adams, visit the following Web sites: http://www.pbs.org/wgbh/amex/ansel and http://www.sfmoma.org/adams.

EXPLORING

○ You will find lots of photography resources in your library or bookstore and on the Internet. Look for information on how to compose photos, arrange lighting, figure camera settings, and choose film for various effects.

○ Photography is a field that you can begin to explore now. Experiment with different cameras and films. Experiment with different kinds of pictures, too. Take photos of friends and family, school events, current events in your town, objects, landscapes, animals, or buildings.

○ Join school camera clubs, or work on your school's yearbook or newspaper staff.

○ Enter contests sponsored by magazines or community groups.

developers and fixers and how to use enlarging equipment. Photographers must also be familiar with the large variety of papers available for printing photographs, all of which deliver a different effect. Most photographers continually experiment with photographic processes to improve their technical proficiency or to create special effects.

Digital photography is a relatively new development. With this new technology, film is replaced by microchips that record pictures in digital format. Pictures can then be downloaded onto a computer's hard drive. Photographers use special software to manipulate the images on screen.

Photographers often specialize in one kind of photography. For example, *portrait photographers* take pictures of people in their own studios, or at schools, homes, weddings, and parties. *Commercial photographers* take pictures of products, fashions, food, or machinery. *Photojournalists* take pictures of events, people, places, or things for newspapers, Internet sites, and magazines. *Aerial photographers* take pictures from airplanes for newspapers, businesses, research companies, or the military. *Scientific photographers* take pictures for scientific magazines and books. *Fine art photographers* take pictures for artistic expression. They might shoot images that are beautiful, thought-provoking, or even disturbing to convey ideas and feelings.

What Do Wildlife Photographers Do?

Wildlife photographers take photographs and make films of animals in their natural environment. Wildlife photographers provide photographs for science publications, research reports, textbooks, newspapers and magazines. Films are used in research and for professional and public education.

Wildlife photographers often find themselves in swamps, deserts, jungles, at the tops of trees, or in underground tunnels, swimming in the ocean, or hanging from the side of a mountain. They may shoot pictures of the tiniest insects or the largest mammals.

Some wildlife photographers specialize in one family or species or in one region or area. For example, some wildlife photographers may shoot chimpanzees in their various habitats around the world. Another photographer might shoot various species of birds that live in the southwestern United States.

The technological advances in photographic equipment and the expertise of wildlife photographers have contributed much to scientific knowledge about animal behavior, new species, evolution, and animals' roles in preserving or changing the environment.

Education and Training: A high school diploma is recommended for this career, and earning a college degree will help you learn about both photography and biology. A bachelor of arts in photography or film with a minor in biology would prepare you well for a career as a wildlife photographer.

Earnings: Full-time wildlife photographers earn average salaries of about $35,000 to $50,000 a year. Most wildlife photographers work as freelancers.

Outlook: Employment of photographers will increase about as fast as the average. The demand for new photographs and videos of animals in their natural habitats should remain strong in research, education, communication, and entertainment.

For more information on this exciting career, contact the North American Nature Photography Association (http://www.nanpa.org)

Education and Training

Classes in photography, chemistry, and art will help prepare you for this career. If you are interested in digital photography, study computers and learn how to use programs that manipulate photos.

To Be a Successful Photographer, You Should . . .

- ○ be creative and imaginative
- ○ have good eyesight and color vision
- ○ have an eye for form and line
- ○ have good business skills if you are self-employed
- ○ be self-motivated
- ○ be able to handle deadline pressure

You do not have to earn a college degree to become a photographer, but many colleges offer a bachelor's degree

FOR MORE INFO

For information on careers for media photographers, contact

American Society of Media Photographers
150 North Second Street
Philadelphia, PA 19106-1912
Tel: 215-451-2767
http://www.asmp.org

This association has a job bank and education information and publishes New Photographer *magazine.*

National Press Photographers Association
3200 Croasdaile Drive, Suite 306
Durham, NC 27705-2588
Tel: 919-383-7246
E-mail: info@nppa.org
http://www.nppa.org

This organization provides training, publishes its own magazine, and offers various services for its members.

Professional Photographers of America
229 Peachtree Street NE, Suite 2200
Atlanta, GA 30303-1608
Tel: 800-786-6277
E-mail: csc@ppa.com
http://www.ppa.com

For information on opportunities in photography for women, contact

Professional Women Photographers
511 Avenue of the Americas, #138
New York, NY 10011-8436
E-mail: info@pwponline.org
http://www.pwponline.org

in photography. A college program will teach you advanced techniques and help you build a portfolio of your work.

Earnings

Salaried photographers earned median salaries of $26,170 in 2006, according to the U.S. Department of Labor. Salaries ranged from less than $15,540 to $56,640 or more. Many photographers are self-employed freelancers. They often earn more than those receiving a salary, but their earnings can go up and down depending on how much work is available.

Outlook

Employment of photographers will increase about as fast as the average, according to the U.S. Department of Labor. The demand for new photographs should remain strong in education, communication, entertainment, marketing, and research. As more newspapers and magazines turn to electronic publishing, it will increase the need for digital photographs. Demand should also increase for photographers who specialize in portraiture, especially of children.

Special Effects Technicians

What Special Effects Technicians Do

Special effects technicians make fantastic things seem real in movies, theater, and television. They can make a spaceship fly to distant planets, perch a car on top of a skyscraper, or bring dinosaurs to life on the screen.

Special effects technicians read scripts and meet with directors to decide on the kinds of effects they will use. Special effects may include computer animation, makeup effects, pyrotechnics, and mechanical effects.

Computer animation specialists use computer programs to create effects that would be impossible or too costly to build. These effects make it possible for a human face to change or "morph" into an animal's face, or for a realistic-looking bear to drink a popular soda.

Makeup effects specialists create masks and costumes. They build prosthetic devices, such as human or animal heads or limbs. They must be skilled at modeling, sewing, applying makeup, and mixing dyes.

Pyrotechnics effects specialists are experts with firearms and explosives. They create explosions for dramatic scenes. This work can be very dangerous. Most states require them to be licensed in order to handle and set off explosives.

Award Winners

These films received Oscars in the category of visual effects:

2006: *Pirates of the Caribbean: Dead Man's Chest*

2005: *King Kong*

2004: *Spider-Man 2*

2003: *The Lord of the Rings: The Return of the King*

2002: *The Lord of the Rings: The Two Towers*

2001: *The Lord of the Rings: The Fellowship of the Ring*

2000: *Gladiator*

1999: *The Matrix*

1998: *What Dreams May Come*

1997: *Titanic*

Mechanical effects specialists build sets, props, and backgrounds. They build, install, and operate equipment mechanically or electrically. They usually are skilled in carpentry, electricity, welding, and robotics.

Education and Training

To be a special effects technician, you need to know about science and art. Take classes in art, sculpture, art history, chemistry, physics, shop, and computers.

Some universities have film and television programs that offer courses in special effects. Most technicians in the industry say that the best way into this career is through experience working on a film crew.

Earnings

A salary survey by the International Alliance of Theatrical Stage Employers, Moving Picture Technicians, Artists, and Allied Crafts shows that employment in digital effects can pay very well, even in assistant positions. The survey found that character animators, CGI effects animators, and art directors earned from $55,000 to $350,000 with an average of about $100,000 a year. Effects assistants had beginning salaries of around $45,000, and median salaries of $60,000 a year.

EXPLORING

- Explore computer animation software programs that allow you to create special effects.
- Visit your school or public library and bookstores to read more about special effects technology. Look for magazines such as *Animation Journal, Cinefex, Daily Variety,* and *Hollywood Reporter.*
- If you have a video camera, experiment with special effects in filming and editing.
- Work on school drama productions as a stagehand, sound technician, or makeup artist. You will learn about set and prop design, and how to use tools and mechanical and electrical equipment.

A makeup effects specialist applies makeup to a mask. (Shelly Gazin, The Image Works)

The Most Influential Visual Effects Films of All Time

1. *Star Wars* (1977)
2. *Blade Runner* (1982)
3. *2001: A Space Odyssey* (1968)
3. *The Matrix* (1999)
5. *Jurassic Park* (1993)
6. *Tron* (1982)
7. *King Kong* (1933)
8. *Close Encounters of the Third Kind* (1977)
9. *Alien* (1979)
10. *The Abyss* (1989)

Source: Visual Effects Society

Outlook

There is strong competition for jobs in this field, and competition will likely increase as the cost of powerful computers and graphics software decreases. More people will be able to develop their own computer animation skills.

FOR MORE INFO

For information about colleges with film and television programs of study, and to read interviews with filmmakers, visit the AFI's Web site.

American Film Institute (AFI)
2021 North Western Avenue
Los Angeles, CA 90027-1657
Tel: 323-856-7600
http://www.afi.com

For extensive information about the digital effects industry, visit the AWN's Web site.

Animation World Network (AWN)
6525 Sunset Boulevard, Garden Suite 10

Hollywood, CA 90028-7212
Tel: 323-606-4200
E-mail: info@awn.com
http://www.awn.com

For information about festivals and presentations, and news about the industry, contact

Visual Effects Society
5535 Balboa Boulevard, Suite 205
Encino, CA 91316-1544
Tel: 818-981-7861
E-mail: info@Visualeffectssociety.com
http://www.visualeffectssociety.com

The competition for jobs in film special effects houses is stiff. For more than 25 years now, films of all kinds have used computer graphics and high-tech effects, inspiring a whole generation of young people with computers and imaginations.

Digital technology will continue to change the industry. Experts predict that within 10 years, film will be completely replaced by digital processes, recording scenes digitally so they can be further enhanced by computer effects.

Glossary

accredited approved as meeting established standards for providing good training and education; this approval is usually given by an independent organization of professionals

apprentice a person who is learning a trade by working under the supervision of a skilled worker; apprentices often receive classroom instruction in addition to their supervised practical experience

associate's degree an academic rank or title granted by a community or junior college or similar institution to graduates of a two-year program of education beyond high school

bachelor's degree an academic rank or title given to a person who has completed a four-year program of study at a college or university; also called an undergraduate degree or baccalaureate

career an occupation for which a worker receives training and has an opportunity for advancement

certified approved as meeting established requirements for skill, knowledge, and experience in a particular field; people are certified by the organization of professionals in their field

college a higher education institution that is above the high school level

community college a public or private two-year college attended by students who do not usually live at the college; graduates of a community college receive an associate's degree and may transfer to a four-year college or university to complete a bachelor's degree

diploma   a certificate or document given by a school to show that a person has completed a course or has graduated from the school

distance education   a type of educational program that allows students to take classes and complete their education by mail or the Internet

doctorate   the highest academic rank or title granted by a graduate school to a person who has completed a two- to three-year program after having received a master's degree

fringe benefit   a payment or benefit to an employee in addition to regular wages or salary; examples of fringe benefits include a pension, a paid vacation, and health or life insurance

graduate school   a school that people may attend after they have received their bachelor's degree; people who complete an educational program at a graduate school earn a master's degree or a doctorate

intern   an advanced student (usually one with at least some college training) in a professional field who is employed in a job that is intended to provide supervised practical experience for the student

internship   (1) the position or job of an intern; (2) the period of time when a person is an intern

junior college   a two-year college that offers courses like those in the first half of a four-year college program; graduates of a junior college usually receive an associate's degree and may transfer to a four-year college or university to complete a bachelor's degree

liberal arts   the subjects covered by college courses that develop broad general knowledge rather than specific occupational skills; the liberal arts are often considered to include philosophy, literature and the arts, history, language, and some courses in the social sciences and natural sciences

major   (in college) the academic field in which a student specializes and receives a degree

master's degree   an academic rank or title granted by a graduate school to a person who has completed a one- or two-year program after having received a bachelor's degree

pension   an amount of money paid regularly by an employer to a former employee after he or she retires from working

scholarship   a gift of money to a student to help the student pay for further education

social studies   courses of study (such as civics, geography, and history) that deal with how human societies work

starting salary   salary paid to a newly hired employee; the starting salary is usually a smaller amount than is paid to a more experienced worker

technical college   a private or public college offering two- or four-year programs in technical subjects; technical colleges offer courses in both general and technical subjects and award associate's degrees and bachelor's degrees

undergraduate   a student at a college or university who has not yet received a degree

undergraduate degree   see **bachelor's degree**

union   an organization whose members are workers in a particular industry or company; the union works to gain better wages, benefits, and working conditions for its members; also called a labor union or trade union

vocational school   a public or private school that offers training in one or more skills or trades

wage   money that is paid in return for work done, especially money paid on the basis of the number of hours or days worked

Index of Job Titles

Browse and Learn More

Books

Brommer, Gerald, and Joseph Gatto. 2d ed. *Careers In Art: An Illustrated Guide*. New York: Sterling Publishing, 1999.

Camenson, Blythe. *Great Jobs for Art Majors*. 2d ed. New York: McGraw-Hill, 2003.

Dubosque, D. C. *Draw 3-D: A Step by Step Guide to Perspective Drawing*. Gilsum, N.H.: Peel Productions, 1998.

Gordon, Barbara. *Opportunities in Commercial Art and Graphic Design Careers*. New York: McGraw-Hill, 2003.

Gulrich, Kathy. *187 Tips for Artists: How to Create a Successful Art Career—and Have Fun in the Process!* 2d ed. New York: Center City Publishing, 2007.

Herbert, Janis. *Leonardo da Vinci for Kids: His Life and Ideas, 21 Activities*. Chicago: Chicago Review Press, 1998.

Phaidon Press. *The Art Book For Children*. Boston: Phaidon Press, 2005.

Raimondo, Joyce. *Imagine That!: Activities and Adventures in Surrealism*. New York: Watson-Guptill Publications, 2004.

Roche, Art. *Art for Kids: Cartooning: The Only Cartooning Book You'll Ever Need to Be the Artist You've Always Wanted to Be*. Asheville, N.C.: Lark Books, 2005.

Salmon, Mark, and Bill Barrett. *Opportunities in Visual Arts Careers*. New York: McGraw-Hill, 2001.

Temple, Kathryn. *Art for Kids: Drawing: The Only Drawing Book You'll Ever Need to Be the Artist You've Always Wanted to Be*. Asheville, N.C.: Lark Books, 2005.

Watt, Fiona, et al. *The Usborne Book of Art Ideas*. London, U.K.: Usborne Publishing, 2004.

Web Sites

The Art Junction
http://www.artjunction.org

About: Art History
http://arthistory.about.com

About: Drawing/Sketching
http://drawsketch.about.com

Albright-Knox ArtGames
http://www.albrightknox.org/artgames

All About Art
http://library.thinkquest.org/J001159/index.htm

Amazing Kids Virtual Art Gallery
http://www.amazing-kids.org/gallery.html

The American Museum of Photography
http://www.photographymuseum.com

ArtCyclopedia
http://www.artcyclopedia.com

The Art Institute of Chicago: Art Access
http://www.artic.edu/artaccess

Fabric Online
http://library.thinkquest.org/C004179

Fine Art Online
http://www.harcourtschool.com/activity/art_line/art_line.html

International Child Art Foundation
http://www.icaf.org/index3.html

SmART Kids
http://smartmuseum.uchicago.edu/smartkids